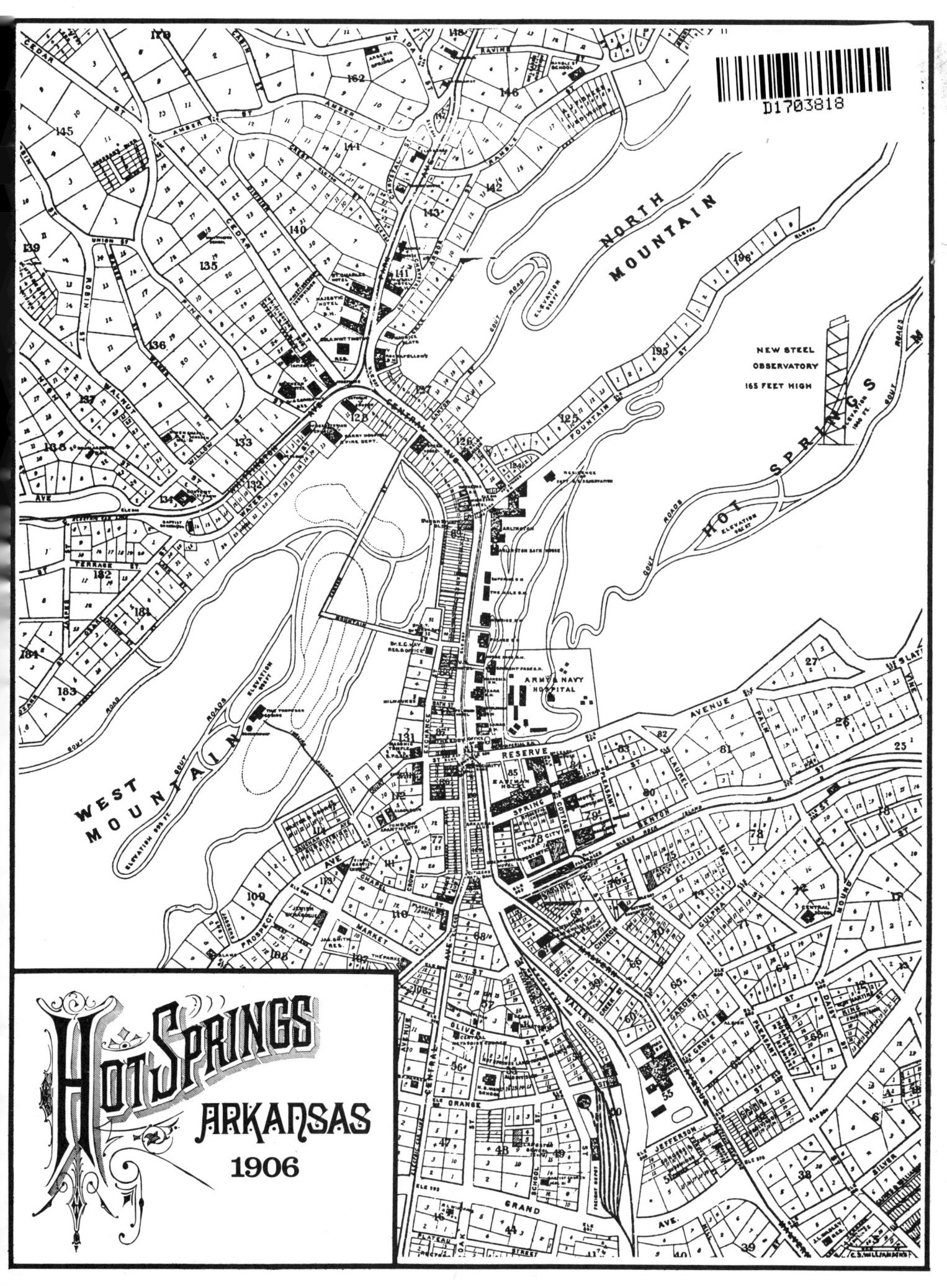

HOT SPRINGS, ARKANSAS

BY DEE BROWN

WHITTINGTON AVENUE.

visual research and design by
DESIGNED COMMUNICATIONS
S. KITTRELL and R.R. WITSELL

ROSE PUBLISHING COMPANY
LITTLE ROCK, ARKANSAS

Books by Dee Brown

Wave High the Banner - 1942
Fighting Indians of the West - 1948
Trail Driving Days - 1952
Grierson's Raid - 1954
The Settler's West - 1955
Yellow Horse - 1956
The Gentle Tamers - 1958
Cavalry Scout - 1958
Bold Cavaliers - 1959
They Went Thataway - 1960
Fort Phil Kearney - 1962
The Galvanized Yankees - 1963
The Girl from Fort Wicked - 1964
Showdown at Little Big Horn - 1964
The Year of the Century: 1876-1966
Action at Beecher Island - 1967
Bury My Heart at Wounded Knee - 1970
Andrew Jackson and the Battle of New Orleans - 1972
Tales of the Warrior Ants - 1973
Hear That Lonesome Whistle Blow - 1977
Creek Mary's Blood - 1980

Library of Congress Catalog Card Number 82-60949
ISBN No. 0-914546-41-4

Copyright 1982 by Dee A. Brown

All rights reserved. This book, or parts thereof, may not be reproduced in any form, except brief excerpts for reviews, without permission in writing from the publisher.

TABLE of CONTENTS

Preface 5

Introduction 7

Chapter I **GENESIS** 9

Chapter II **PILGRIMS** 17

Chapter III **THE AMERICAN SPA** ... 27

Chapter IV **AMENITIES** 45

Chapter V **INHABITANTS** 79

Chapter VI **SOJOURNERS** 89

Index 96

PREFACE

150 years ago, on April 20, 1832, President Andrew Jackson signed the first law in American history to preserve land for recreational purposes. That land was the area which is now known as Hot Springs, Arkansas. What has occurred here since 1832 is nothing less than a compact history of the United States, a fascinating story well worth documenting.

1982, in addition to being the Reservation's 150th Birthday, also marks the 75th Anniversary of the Arkansas Bank and Trust Company of Hot Springs, one of the community's most venerable institutions. This volume was commissioned by Arkansas Bank and Trust to be presented as a birthday gift to the town which has allowed the bank to flourish.

Happy Birthday Hot Springs. We hope you enjoy reading and learning from this book as much as we enjoy providing it.

Arkansas Bank and Trust Company

INTRODUCTION

This history is based mainly upon research done by members of the Garland County Historical Society and published in *The Record* over the past quarter of a century. Without the broad range of subjects covered by Mary D. Hudgins, Inez Cline and others, months of research would have been required to assemble the material used herein. Hot Springs National Park is a city out of which many books can come. Examples are the story of horse racing so ably begun by Peggy Maddox in the 1972 *Record*, and the story of casino gambling initiated by Mary D. Hudgins's "The Flynn-Doran Battle" in the 1973 *Record*.

Other sources most often consulted were files of the *Arkansas Historical Quarterly*, the *Hot Springs Sentinel-Record*, *Arkansas Gazette* and *Arkansas Democrat*.

Especially helpful were the following: Chronologies of Hot Springs prepared by Mary D. Hudgins and Jean Ledwidge, Librarian of the Tri-Lakes Regional Library; Personalities in Hot Springs history assembled by Jean Ledwidge; "The First 150 Years," by Inez Cline; "Hot Springs in the Territorial Period: Early Settlement of the Spa," by Wendy Richter; the reprint of Stephen Crane's newspaper piece, "The Merry Throng at Hot Springs," in the 1980 *Record*; various editions of Cutter's *Guide to Hot Springs*; "Hot Springs: Ante-Bellum Watering Place," by Ruth Irene Jones, *Arkansas Historical Quarterly*, Vol. XIV, 1955, pp. 3-31; "Hot Springs in the 'Seventies," edited by Jerrell H. Shofner and William Warner Rogers, *A.H.Q.*, Vol. XXII, 1963, pp. 24-48; "Sarah Ellsworth, Maker of Arkansas History," by Mary D. Hudgins, *A.H.Q.*, Vol. XI, 1952, pp. 102-112; "The Hot Springs of Arkansas, 1878," by A. Van Cleef, *Harper's Monthly*, January 1878; and that storehouse of information, *Hot Springs Arkansas, and Hot Springs National Park*, by Francis J. Scully, 1966.

In addition to those persons named above, obligations are owed to Russell Baker, Arkansas History Commission; Walter Nunn of Rose Publishing Company; Kirby Williams of the Arkansas Bank and Trust Company; Roger Giddings, Superintendent of Hot Springs National Park; the reference staff of Tri-Lakes Regional Library, and Linda L. Brown, research assistant. The illustrations, many of which have never been published before, were assembled by Suzanne Kittrell and Rebecca Rogers Witsell of Designed Communications. They also created the design for the book. Illustrations from the Garland County Historical Society were provided through the efforts of Inez E. Cline, historian.

The narrative that follows is not chronological, but is told by topics in hopes that a mixture of the years will help readers see how closely the present is related to the long ago, the recent, and only yesterday—and thus perceive that history is by no means dry-as-dust, but is a vital part of our daily lives.

CHAPTER I
GENESIS

"It tasted like Spicewood Tea."

Above: "View at break of day from Hot Springs Mountain" from *America's Baden-Baden Illustrated* published 1880. (Mary D. Hudgins Collection)

Right: Hot Springs Creek with rising steam. (Hot Springs National Park)

No one knows in what epoch the springs began to flow, bubbling with steam from the rocks. Nor do we know when the Indians first found these waters, but they surely viewed them with joy, for sweatbaths were universal among the native Americans, as important as food, shelter and clothing. Sweatbathing was a religious ceremony during which prayers were offered. The ritual also was important in tribal medical practice for the cure of certain diseases; it was hygienic as well as invigorating for those exhausted after arduous hunts and battles.

In the valley of the hot springs it was unnecessary to dig holes and carry water to pour over tediously heated stones. The hot water and its vapors were already there, provided by some benevolent spirit, and the Indians came from the four directions, following streams and animal traces mile after mile. Tunica, Quapaw, Osage, Natchez, and several divisions of the Caddo, and others whose tribal names we can never know, all made the pilgrimage. Friends and enemies met there to rejuvenate body and psyche. Legend tells us they made the valley a neutral ground, the war hatchet permanently buried between the green mountains.

On the high ridges, however, the tribes warred for control of massive beds of novaculite, a siliceous rock more valuable than gold to them because it could be quarried and chipped into tools

and weapons with edges and points harder than steel. These products of Stone Age man could be traded throughout the heartland for other valuable objects. Whatever tribe controlled the hard stone fared well. According to a creation myth of the Caddos, the first members of that tribe issued full-formed from the hot springs. They flourished as tool and weapon traders and then spread southward to the Red River and the Brazos.

In 1541 the first Europeans found the valley. Hernando De Soto and his surviving conquistadors—almost defeated by swamps and cane-brakes—floundered alongside the Mississippi and Arkansas. Perhaps they learned of the springs from peaceable Indians pitying their wretched condition. We can only imagine their wonder and delight at the first vision of vapors rising against the chill air of autumn. They must have quickly cast aside shields and lances and shed their helmets and armor for the first refreshing bath in months.

To place the conquistadors at the springs we have the testimony of one chronicler of the expedition, who called himself "the Gentleman of Elvas." He told of how they camped for a month in a mountainous region, men and horses recuperating after the strenuous summer. "In this time," he wrote, "the horses fattened and throve more than they had done at other places." He credited their restoration to the Indian corn plant. "The blade of it, I think, is the best fodder that grows." And then he added: "The beasts drank so copiously from the very warm and brackish lake, that they came in having their bellies swollen with the leaves, when they came back from their watering . . ."

Where else would they have found "very warm" waters in that area other than at the hot springs? And the word "lake" translated from Portuguese could have been a small pond from a spring. The mystery is why the Spaniards did not make winter camp in that protected valley instead of hacking their way down the Ouachita River to the latter-day sites of Camden, or Calion, or the mouth of the Saline. They would have been much more comfortable at the springs, with hot mineral water for drinking and bathing. But De Soto and his lieutenants rarely exhibited any sensible judgment during their entire expedition. Their madness for gold had made them foolish. Or perhaps the Indians who claimed the area made it clear that Spaniards were not welcome there for an extended stay.

None of the Indians who saw these strange white-skinned intruders could have lived long enough to see the next visitors from the East. They would be Frenchmen, trappers working their way up the Ouachita to search for furs and bear oil, which were more highly prized in New Orleans than hog lard or butter. The French left vestiges of their presence here and there in place names. When William Dunbar and George Hunter came to the hot springs in December 1804, they found an abandoned log cabin and a few split-board shelters that may have been built by the trappers, or by French and Spanish plantation owners who had come to take the baths.

Until 1803 the springs had been a part of the alternate territorial claims of Spain and France, but in that year Napoleon Bonaparte, hard up for cash, offered to sell France's half billion acres of America to President Thomas Jefferson for thirteen million dollars. Recognizing a bargain, Jefferson hastily sealed the deal. The springs and their environs, like the rest of the vast Louisiana Territory, cost the United States about three cents an acre.

Even before the transaction was completed, Jefferson began organizing expeditions to explore the unknown lands. Lewis and Clark's journey to the Pacific Ocean was the most spectacular, but

Above: Indians at the Hot Springs from *Tourist's Souvenir of Hot Springs*. (Mary D. Hudgins Collection)

Below: William Dunbar. (Mary D. Hudgins Collection)

there were others. The President had heard of the hot springs from a friend in Natchez, Mississippi—William Dunbar, a planter and amateur scientist. Jefferson asked Dunbar to lead an expedition into the Ouachita Mountains and report on the Indian tribes, minerals, flora and fauna, and the legendary hot springs. To assist in scientific matters, Dunbar enlisted Dr. George Hunter, a Pennsylvanian who had been trained as a chemist. The other members of the expedition consisted of a dozen soldiers detached from the New Orleans garrison.

As they approached the springs from the site of present-day Malvern they encountered great flocks of wild turkeys. On the afternoon of December 5, one of the soldiers shot twice at a buffalo, but the animal escaped. When they were nine miles from the springs, rain began beating down, and tents had to be pitched at Caulker's (Gulpha?) Creek. Next morning Dunbar sent some of the soldiers ahead to set up camp at the hot springs. On the 8th this party returned, "each giving his own account of the wonderful things he had seen; they were unable to keep the finger a moment in the water as it issued from the rock, they drank of it after cooling a little and found it very agreeable; some of them thinking that it tasted like spice-wood tea."

At dawn the following day, Dunbar and Hunter set out for the springs, encountering higher hills and finding the timber to be chiefly oak with a scattering of pines. For their visit the explorers had chosen one of the coldest winters on record. Snow and freezing rain hindered their work, but on Christmas Day the soldiers were granted a holiday. In expectation of the occasion they had "hoarded up their rations of whiskey, to be expended in merriment on this occasion, which terminated with inebriety but no ill consequences ensued. We amused ourselves with further experiments on the hot waters; the conduct of the analysis being left to Doctor Hunter as a professional chemist . . ."

December 30th was the coldest day they had experienced, nine degrees above zero; the sky was a dark Prussian blue, the stars shining with "uncommon lusture." They prepared to return down the Ouachita, and on January 8, 1805, they reluctantly left the warm waters of the spring. They had not come to stay but to observe, yet the reports of what Dunbar and Hunter had found eventually reached the eyes and ears of others who would come to stay and build a town around the springs that "tasted like spice-wood tea."

Two years later Jean Emanuel Prudhomme, the ailing owner of a Red River plantation, heard about the springs' healing powers from some Natchitoches Indians. The Natchitoches, a division of the Caddo tribe, guided Prudhomme to his destination over the Natchitoches Trace, which had been created by many years of travel between the springs and the trading post that is now Natchitoches, Louisiana.

Prudhomme evidently was pleased by what he found. He built a house, the first real home at the springs, and lived there off and on for two years. Before he departed he was joined by a pair of rugged trappers from Alabama, Isaac Cates and John Percival (sometimes spelled in the records as Persiful and Piercifull.) Cates built himself a wooden trough in one of the springs so that he could lie there and let the warm water lave his body as it flowed past. A restless man, he spent much of his time at fur trapping in the mountains to the west.

Percival, however, saw a great future in the springs. He cleared a farm on Sulphur Creek and raised some of the Indian corn that had been so much admired two and a half centuries earlier by the Gentleman of Elvas. Percival also acquired Prud-

Below: Falls of the Ouachita River from *Harper's New Monthly Magazine*, January 1878. (Mary D. Hudgins Collection)

Above: Hot Springs valley as it appeared to George Featherstonhaugh. (Hot Springs National Park)

Above: Portrait of Jean Emanuel Prudhomme painted in Paris. (Prudhomme family, Natchitoches, Louisiana)

Below: Ludovicus Belding, painted by John Byrd. (Arkansas History Commission)

homme's house when the planter returned to Natchitoches, and he built a few log cabins to rent to the ever-increasing number of visitors to the springs. The upheavals caused by the War of 1812 brought a group of travelers seeking a sanctuary. Among them was Sarah Lemon, who eventually became Percival's wife. Together they opened a boarding house, but when George Featherstonhaugh, a traveling Englishman, stopped there in 1834, he was rather critical of the offered fare—pork swimming in hog's grease, some very badly made bread, and much worse coffee. "They knew very well that we had no other place to go, and had prepared accordingly . . . Percival, however, was a good-natured man, could talk about things that interested us, and promised to look up some venison for another time . . ."

Of others who came in the early years, we know the names of only a few and most of them were travelers who took the trouble to record their impressions before going on their ways. In 1816, an official report to the governor of the Missouri Territory listed only thirteen families living near the springs. The Methodists, who introduced itinerant preachers to the frontier, were represented by the Reverend William Stevens in 1814, and six years later there were enough people to assign a regular circuit rider to the community. After visits in 1822 and 1823, the Reverend John Scripps reported that he held meetings at "Warm Springs" for two or three days, and that fifty to one hundred people camped there "in the summer months for the benefits resulting from bathing in and drinking the water."

Another government representative, Major Stephen Long of the Army's Topographical Engineers, paid a visit in January 1818, and reported finding sixty separate hot springs and fourteen or fifteen rude cabins. He estimated that Hot Springs Creek, formed by the springs and running southward, carried about a thousand gallons a minute.

In 1820, Joseph and Nancy Mellard built the first of the many hostelries that before the end of the century would distinguish Hot Springs as a city of hotels. Up to that time the Percivals had rented cabins and provided meals, but the Mellards operated their dog-trot log cabin as a hotel, with enough beds and utensils to serve a considerable number of guests.

Eight years later, however, Mellard died, and but for the arrival of a family from faraway Massachusetts the fledgling hotel business probably would have languished. Ludovicus Belding with his wife and children rolled into the community in a wagon, probably canvas-covered, in 1828. For a few months they lived in one of Percival's cabins, but eventually Belding built a hotel that was comfortable enough to win high compliments from a Little Rock newspaper. "Good food, clean linen, silver forks and spoons, much attention to guests and moderate charges, entitle Mr. Belding to encouragement." Belding's son George, born in 1832, had the distinction of being the first white child whose birthplace was Hot Springs. George Belding's son, George R., served as Mayor from 1898 to 1906.

Every town or city that amounts to anything usually owes its dynamism to one or two individuals whose drive, imagination and determination galvanize others into action. Such a man was Hiram Abiff Whittington. In 1826 he journeyed to Arkansas from Boston, Massachusetts, as a young man of twenty-one to join William Woodruff in publishing the *Arkansas Gazette* in Little Rock, but a visit to Hot Springs in 1832 led to his becoming a permanent resident. Directly across the creek from the springs he built a store from which he supplied the few hundred inhabitants of what was then Hot Springs County. Barter was the usual method of trade. "We have no money here and never had," he wrote his brother in Boston. "Our business is all done in cotton and skins." He also accepted beans and bear oil.

Whittington was a lover of books, and he ordered so many from Boston that he soon had a sizable library in one corner of his

Right: Hot Springs Creek c. 1860. (Arkansas History Commission)

store. Wishing to spread the benefits of reading among his neighbors, he allowed books to be borrowed and therefore must receive credit for establishing what must have been the first circulating library in the Territory. When George Featherstonhaugh visited the springs in 1834, Whittington was the first man he met. The merchant, Featherstonhaugh noted, "was obliging enough to say we might take possession of one of the log cabins . . . and through our new friend [we] got skins, blankets and other appliances to serve as bedding."

During his long residence in Hot Springs, Whittington later built a hotel, served as postmaster, held several local offices, and represented his district in the Arkansas legislature. As was true in most frontier areas, eligible unmarried women were in short supply. "I have some notion of going up among the Cherokees," he wrote to his brother. Although he was impressed by the charm and beauty of the Cherokee girls he met at Dwight Mission, Whittington finally solved his problem by returning to Boston on a visit. There he found a wife, Mary Burnham, and brought her back to Hot Springs. He died in 1890, on the eve of his town's glorious Gay Nineties era. Today the Hotel Majestic stands on the site of the old Whittington home.

Below: Residence of Hiram Whittington from *Cutter's Guide to the Hot Springs of Arkansas*, 1887. (Mary D. Hudgins Collection)

Above: Hiram Abiff Whittington. (Mary D. Hudgins Collection)

Below: Ambrose H. Sevier. (Arkansas History Commission)

Like many another frontier community Hot Springs had a difficult time getting started as a proper town. Ludovicus Belding tried to name it Thermopolis, and for a few years in the 1820's some people persisted in calling the place Warm Springs. The first post office, established in December 1829, bore that name, and it was more than a year later before the bureaucrats in Washington got around to changing the town and county names back to Hot Springs. The post office could not have been a very busy one. The 1830 census lists only 84 people living in the township, 438 in the county. Thanks to Arkansas's territorial delegate to Congress, Ambrose Sevier, the community received a boost toward permanence in 1832 when his bill set aside four sections of land as a federal reservation "with the Hot Springs as near the center as may be . . . and are not to be entered, pre-empted or appropriated for any purpose whatever." President Andrew Jackson signed the

Above: U. S. Senator Solon Borland. (Arkansas History Commission)

Below: Henry Massie Rector. (Mary D. Hudgins Collection)

bill on April 20, and made it into law; it was the first time the Federal Government chose to preserve land for recreational purposes.

Not until January 10, 1851, however, was the town incorporated, and by that time the Hot Springs County seat had been transferred to Rockport (later Malvern), and not until after Garland County was formed in 1873 did Hot Springs have a courthouse again. In 1875, following the Civil War, the town was re-incorporated.

In the meantime the community had attracted many new residents. The 1850 census listed 3,669 inhabitants of Hot Springs County—3,237 whites, 361 slaves, and eleven free colored. A breakdown of occupations for Hot Springs township in that year serves as a mirror of daily life in the burgeoning town itself: Four hundred farmers, three hundred laborers, thirteen carpenters, twelve teachers, eleven blacksmiths, eleven grocers, seven merchants, seven tanners, six millers, five doctors, three stage drivers, three tavern keepers, two preachers, two lawyers, two saddlers, a bootmaker, chain-maker, cooper, tailor, river pilot, surveyor, wheelwright, gunsmith, sheriff and a U.S. Senator (Solon Borland). Ten years later the town itself had 201 permanent residents, but the beginning of the Civil War was only months away, a cataclysm that would change everything before it ended and come very close to destroying all the bright dreams of those who would make Hot Springs into one of the world's great watering places.

The outbreak of the Civil War in 1861 had little effect upon life in the isolated town until the following spring. In March of 1862 a Federal army defeated the Confederates at Pea Ridge and shortly afterward the Confederate forces withdrew across the Mississippi, leaving the state capital at Little Rock open to capture. After Union troops occupied Batesville in April, Governor Henry M. Rector decided to remove himself and the state's important papers to a safer place. Being a former resident of Hot Springs and owner of a hotel there, he chose that as his haven. On May 6 he ordered his adjutant-general to raise as many volunteers as possible and use them to impede the progress of the Federal army towards the capital. Then he packed up the most important records and—with the state treasurer and funds—journeyed to Hot Springs. Rector's political enemies taunted him for his lack of coolness, and although he returned the seat of government to Little Rock in July, he lost his office in an election later in the year.

Rector's action, however, was a forerunner of events to come. A year later (September 11, 1863) Union forces did seize Little Rock, and Rector's successor, Governor Harris Flanagin, fled southward. According to an account of a Confederate soldier, Charles T. Anderson, at least some of the state records were still in Hot Springs. "The Yanks and Jayhawkers got into Hot Springs and were destroying everything," he wrote. "Our regiment was ordered to the Springs to get what books and papers we could find. We went by way of Caddo Gap through the mountains, and arrived at the Springs late one evening. We gathered up what papers we could find and traveled all night with the Yankees after us. We brought the papers to Washington." And it was there, some sixty miles southwest of Hot Springs that the Arkansas state government remained until the war's end.

Late in 1863, units of the 3rd Iowa Union Cavalry under Lieutenant-Colonel H. C. Caldwell patrolled from Benton to Caddo Gap and Mount Ida, but in the official records of the war only one skirmish is recorded at Hot Springs, on February 4, 1864. A Confederate company led by Captain William Harrison inflicted casualties upon a band of guerrillas who had been raiding through the area.

By that time most of the able-bodied men had marched away to war, leaving the community defenseless. Many families had fled to Texas or Louisiana, and during their absence bushwhackers burned abandoned houses. Some reports indicate that only three families remained to the end. They included the widow of William Chase, who had come to the valley in 1839. "Grandma" Chase, she was called, and when guerrillas threatened she would sit defiantly on her front porch with a shotgun across her lap.

One highly prized item in the area during the war was a powder made from deposits of a soft rocklike substance that could be found at Mountain Valley's Soda Spring. It was used as a substitute for yeast powders, unobtainable after Little Rock fell to Union forces.

Unlike many Arkansas towns of promise that withered forever during that devastating war, Hot Springs revived rapidly. The exiles returned from Texas and Louisiana, rebuilt on the ashes of their homes, and began opening new stores, hotels, houses, and bath houses. The key to future prosperity, of course, was the presence of the thermal springs, and it became evident by the early 1870's that some permanent legal decision must be made as to whether they should be privately or publicly owned.

Although Congress had formed a federal reservation around the springs in 1832, various individuals still laid claim to tracts of land which encompassed them. They included the Rector family, John C. Hale, who had purchased land rights from the Percivals, and the heirs of Ludovicus Belding, represented by Major William H. Gaines, a son-in-law. These claimants, according to a contemporary observer, were well known to visitors as well as to citizens. "Their various claims, their well-known hostility to each other, and each new expression of it form a staple subject of conversation among the visitors. First there is 'ex-Gov. Rector,' Governor of the State at the time of the war, who made the well-known profane concise telegraphic reply in response to President Lincoln's call for troops; ("Hell, no!" according to legend), then comes old Major Gaines, with his bevy of daughters; last, but not least, if he is crippled, is 'Old Man Hale,' as he is called, who rejoices in the honor of having been shot seventeen times in 'personal encounters,' as they are delicately termed in Arkansas."

After a long period of litigation, the U.S. Supreme Court decided on April 24, 1876, that none of the claimants held a valid right to the springs, and declared Hot Springs Reservation to be under federal control. On March 3, 1877, the government ordered an official survey of the reservation. To protect persons who were already established, Congress empowered a commission to assign rights and compensation case by case to those who were judged to have made reasonable property commitments.

Although individual legal suits continued for some years, the way was now open for the growth of a city whose main purpose would be to provide attractive and desirable services for visitors who would come from all across the nation in search of health and pleasurable recreation.

Above: Residence of "Grand-ma" Chase from *Hot Springs Illustrated Monthly*, 1879. (Walter Nunn Collection)

Below: Major William H. Gaines from *Centennial History of Arkansas* by Dallas Herndon. (Charles Witsell, Jr.)

CHAPTER II

"All Roads of Every Kind Terminate at the Hot Springs"

From the earliest days until after the Civil War, Hot Springs was not an easy place for visitors to reach. Only the most determined of travelers made the journey over rough and dangerous trails, at first on horseback, then in wagons or buggies, and after 1836 in stagecoaches of dubious comfort. "Few invalids were equal to the hardships and fatigue of such a journey," one visitor commented, and yet the ailing were the ones who most wanted to come to benefit from the healing springs.

During Arkansas's territorial era, travel was mainly by steamboat. As the Ouachita was barely navigable by small boats so far north as Hot Springs, visitors had to journey there by land. The first roads across the territory were laid out by the federal government for use of troop movements to the farther western frontier, and were called military roads. Later on the Post Office added other routes that were known as post roads. The closest military road to Hot Springs ran southwest from Little Rock to Washington and then to Fulton on the Red River. It was generally known as the Southwest Trail, and visitors from the north turned off near Magnet Cove, as George Featherstonhaugh did in December 1834 when he was traveling by wagon. "An obscure track that led to . . . the Hot Springs," he recorded. "For the first

Above: Along the Iron Mountain Route, St. Louis to Hot Springs, Arkansas, from *America's Baden-Baden Illustrated*, 1880. (Mary D. Hudgins Collection)

Below: Stage office and George Belding's store c. 1880. (Garland Co. Historical Society)

three miles the country rose, and the road became exceedingly rocky and difficult; added to which the mountain streams were beginning to assume a fierce character that rendered them dangerous, concealing rocks which often were on the point of overturning us . . . we had to pass some violent streams, especially one called the Gulfer (Gulpha) which we achieved with some difficulty; at length, coming near a ridge, we turned into a narrow passage or vale between the lofty hills, and saw from the appearance of things that we had reached the Hot Springs of the Washita, so much the curiosity to men of science, and so little known to the world."

For travelers from the south there was a trail that turned off the military road at Greenville, a settlement a few miles west of present-day Arkadelphia. Later it was developed into a post road, and mail between Hot Springs and Little Rock went by this roundabout route. "All roads of every kind terminate at the Hot Springs," Featherstonhaugh declared. "Beyond them there is nothing but the unbroken wilderness, the tracks and fords of which are only known to a few hunters."

Some improvement in travel began in 1836 when scheduled stagecoaches replaced the irregular hack service and two-horse carriages provided by Little Rock livery stables. By 1838, "elegant Troy coaches," which were lighter but similar in design to the famed Concords, were meeting river packets at various landings on the Arkansas and White rivers and taking their passengers from New Orleans and Memphis directly to Hot Springs. Even so, travelers sometimes had to get out of the coaches and walk up steep hills or over places where it was so rough the vehicles were in danger of overturning. In the 1840's, stagecoaches required two days to make the trip between Hot Springs and Little Rock. They departed at daylight, and the fare was six dollars each way. So little improvement was made in the roads, however, that in 1862 when Governor Rector removed the state records from Little Rock to Hot Springs, he sent them by boat up the Arkansas River to Dardanelle and then overland the remainder of the way.

By the 1870's—that swashbuckling decade of violence that followed the Civil War—a new hazard arose for travelers on the roads to the Springs. Shortly after three o'clock on the afternoon of January 15, 1874, a stagecoach accompanied by two light road wagons (known as ambulances) reached the Gaines place about five miles from their Hot Springs destination. The Gaines family cemetery can still be seen today from the Malvern highway. Here as was customary, they halted to water horses. During the brief stop, five horsemen wearing heavy blue army overcoats approached from the direction of Hot Springs. They nodded casually to the drivers and passed by. After the stagecoach and ambulances had moved on about half a mile, the horsemen reappeared from the rear, the leader shouting at the coach driver: "Stop, or we'll blow your head off!"

George R. Crump, a Memphis tobacco salesman en route to the Springs, raised the curtain over his coach window and found himself facing a pointed pistol. "Get out quick!" was the order, followed by loud profanity, and he quickly obeyed. Outside, three of the blue-coated highwaymen stood in a row, their pistols cocked; the fourth man was off the one side with a shotgun at the ready; the fifth was on the opposite side of the vehicles. "Walking armories," was the way George Crump later described them.

After ordering the thirty or so passengers out of the three vehicles, the outlaws formed them into a circle and began collecting watches, jewelry, and money from them. In addition to

Right: Scenes on the "Gulpher" from *Hot Springs Illustrated Monthly*, 1879. (Walter Nunn Collection)

Below: 1836 stage advertisement from the Centennial Edition of the *Arkansas Gazette*, 1936. (Arkansas Gazette)

Above: The Malvern and Hot Springs stage from *Hot Springs, Arkansas, The Carlsbad of America*, 1893. (Hot Springs National Park)

Right: "The Arkansas Traveller" from *Harper's New Monthly Magazine*, January 1878. (Mary D. Hudgins Collection)

Crump, the passengers included Governor John Burbank of the Dakota Territory. Because Hot Springs had no banks at that time, visitors coming to take extended thermal treatments had to bring large sums of cash, and the robbers knew this. From Governor Burbank they took $840, a diamond pin, and a gold watch. Similar sums of money were taken from a New Yorker and a man from Massachusetts.

As soon as the outlaws' leader completed rounding the circle, he asked if any of the victims had served in the Confederate Army. Crump replied that he had done so. "What command?" the robber demanded. Crump evidently satisfied his interrogator; his watch and money were returned to him. The others were not so fortunate. The robbers used harsh words against a correspondent for the St. Louis *Democrat*, a newspaper that supported President Grant's administration (then in power) and Reconstruction in the South. The leader accused the reporter of writing for "the vilest paper in the West," and then remarked offhandedly: "I bet I can shoot his hat off without touching a hair of his head." He made no effort to try this, however, and turned to the New Yorker and New Englander, condemning them because they were Yankees. Now they must pay, he said, because they had brought devastation to the South, driving good men into outlawry.

It was not easy for the tense victims to determine whether the robbers were bantering with them or being serious. Their occasional jollity was more disturbing than reassuring. When Governor Burbank asked if he might have his personal papers returned, the outlaw kneeled down to examine them. Suddenly he stood erect, still flipping through the papers, and stared hard at Burbank. "Boys, I believe he's a detective," he said. "Shoot him." Three pistols were immediately turned on Burbank. "Whoa," the leader drawled, "I guess he's all right." And with a smile he handed the governor his papers.

Next he turned to the man from Syracuse, New York, who looked as if he needed a long cure at the Springs. The robber studied him for a minute, and then handed the man a five-dollar bill, advising him to use it to telegraph home for replenishment of his stolen funds. The five highwaymen then departed the scene of the holdup and rode on to Malvern where observers later reported seeing them partake of a leisurely breakfast on the following morning. That was the last seen of them for a while, but almost everyone involved was certain the men were from the Missouri

Above: Jesse James. (Mary D. Hudgins Collection)

Above: Cole Younger. (Mary D. Hudgins Collection)

Below: Jim Younger. (Mary D. Hudgins Collection)

Below: Bob Younger. (Mary D. Hudgins Collection)

Ozarks. A correspondent for the *Arkansas Gazette* coyly described the leader as "a Missouri brigand whose name we forget" with a ten thousand dollar reward on his head—a round-about identification of Jesse James.

About eight months later, September 18, 1874, Sarah Ellsworth of Hot Springs wrote in a letter: "Another robbery of the hack occurred last night about ten miles out of town." She blamed the holdup on the James-Younger gang. "They took the horses from the hack and left their Indian ponies. There were about sixteen passengers in all and the thieves got about $1,000.00."

Although this second robbery occurred in darkness, the bandits wore no masks, and the drivers for the El Paso Stage Lines operating between Hot Springs and Malvern were confident that at least two of them participated in the first robbery. Five stages and hacks traveling some distance apart were stopped one by one. Each time the robbers unhitched the horses and extinguished the oil lamps on the vehicles. As soon as all passengers were assembled outside, they were relieved of their weapons, which were then unloaded and tossed in a pile at the foot of a nearby tree.

Passengers described two of the holdup men as being large with sandy beards, the other two short and thickset. When the robbers were satisfied they had collected all the desired valuables, they broke open a box of grapes and shared them with the passengers. Then they abandoned the skinny mustangs they were riding and transferred their saddles to four of the stageline's best

Above: Hot Springs valley looking south c. 1865. (Hot Springs Chamber of Commerce)

Above: "Glimpses of the Gulpha" from *Hot Springs, Arkansas, The Carlsbad of America*, 1893. (Hot Springs National Park)

Left: Advertisement for the Iron Mountain Route from *Cutter's Guide to the Hot Springs of Arkansas*, 1882. (Mary D. Hudgins Collection)

horses. As they rode away, one of the highwaymen motioned to the pile of empty firearms beside the tree. "Better take your guns," he said. "You might meet robbers on this road."

As soon as the delayed caravan of stages and hacks reached Hot Springs, Colonel John Bartholomew, superintendent of the El Paso line, and John Sumpter, Garland County's sheriff, organized a posse of twenty men and started pursuit. California Jack Gillis, an old Indian fighter living in Hot Springs for his health, served as tracker. Although the posse pursued with vigor, first toward Murfreesboro and then through Amity and Caddo Gap—coming close enough at one time to wound one of the pursued—the outlaws finally managed to work their way through the Ouachita Mountains and across the line into the sanctuary of Indian Territory.

Dime novel authors and serious biographers later identified the Hot Springs stagecoach robbers as Jesse James and Frank James, Cole and Bob Younger, and Clell Miller. When Cole Younger was undergoing his rehabilitation period in prison, he denied being involved in either of the Hot Springs stagecoach robberies, but during a remunerative speaking tour in 1909, he gave a lecture in the Springs on November 27, and admitted participating.

The stagecoach and hack lines that suffered at the hands of the James-Younger gang in 1874 were one of the town's connections with the St. Louis, Iron Mountain & Southern Railway which ran twenty miles to the east of Hot Springs, and had just been completed to Texarkana—the only railroad then operating south of the Arkansas River. Stagecoaches met the passenger trains at Rockport (Malvern) and were "always in readiness to convey passengers over a rough rocky road to the Springs."

In July 1873 a visitor noted that various citizens of Hot Springs expressed the hope to him that before another year rolled around they would not only be "in communication with the outside world by stage and hack lines but that the iron horse with its shrill whistle would be heard throughout these valleys and mountain tops."

Thanks to an enterprising Yankee, this dream of the citizens came to reality two years later. Joseph Reynolds was a New Yorker who had moved to Chicago before the Civil War to make a fortune at tanning hides. By the end of the 1870's he was buying and selling grain and had expanded into the booming steamboat business on the Mississippi and its tributaries. His boats flew a diamond-shaped ensign bearing the letters JO. He stamped the same insignia upon his leather goods. "Diamond Jo" Reynolds probably could be classified as a minor Robber Baron of the Gilded Age, keeping company with the likes of the Vanderbilts, Carnegies, Goulds, and Rockefellers. When rheumatism struck him in 1874, Reynolds decided to visit Hot Springs and take the cure. He rode a Pullman car in reasonable comfort on the rails of the Iron Mountain to Malvern, but there he had to transfer to a hack in order to reach the Spa and its soothing waters. After two or three hours of jerks and bumps and many jolts and jostles from the rocky road, the hack was forced to stop for repairs. Some stories say that Diamond Jo and two of his companions, impatient from the delay, decided to walk the remaining distance, but this seems unlikely because of his physical condition. Others say he spent the night in a farm house, quarreling with the driver while the repairs were being made. At any rate, the experience led to his building a connecting railway from Malvern to Hot Springs. After taking the baths, he knew he would be returning regularly in the future, and he was a man who liked his comforts and conveniences, and could afford them.

Disdaining the customary land grants, government bonds and sale of stock, Reynolds paid for his railroad's construction with his own money, keeping costs down by making it narrow-gauge (three feet between rails). David A. Butterfield, a veteran stagecoach line operator in the West, supervised construction; the town of Butterfield was named for him. Although officially listed as Hot Springs Railroad, it was affectionately called the "Diamond Jo" by citizens of the town. Its tracks stopped beside the Iron Mountain's station at Malvern so that passengers could walk across a roofed platform from one train to another. Although the Diamond Jo train was drawn by a simple woodburning locomotive with a flared smokestack, Reynolds outfitted his passenger cars with the best

Above: Diamond Jo Reynolds. (Mary D. Hudgins Collection)

Below: Invalids changing trains at the Malvern Junction from *Hot Springs Illustrated Monthly*, 1879. (Walter Nunn Collection)

Above: Wood-burning locomotive of the Hot Springs Railroad. (Mary D. Hudgins Collection)

Below: Hot Springs Street Railroad advertisement from *Hot Springs Illustrated Monthly*, 1879. (Walter Nunn Collection)

HOT SPRINGS
Street Railroad.

Cars run the entire length of the Valley, passing all the hotels and bath houses. Carry passengers to and from all trains on the Narrow Gauge Railroad. Fare, 5 tickets for 25 cents. Single fare, 10 cents.

S. W. FORDYCE,
President.
J. L. BUTTERFIELD, Supt.

furnishings of the time—fine interior wood paneling, leather upholstered seats, silk curtains and velvet drapes. Because of the locomotive's small tender, a fresh supply of wood had to be loaded on at Magnet, and if Reynolds was riding the train he would usually lead his wealthy friends off to help the fireman toss billets aboard.

Upon arrival in Hot Springs, passengers disembarked at a small depot at Cottage and Benton Streets and there they could hire a carriage or climb aboard a mule-driven streetcar which moved quietly over a rail line that ran the entire length of Valley Street (Central Avenue), passing all the leading hotels and bath houses. To add sound effects to the ride, the drivers cracked their whips vigorously, and bells attached to the mules' harness jingled constantly to announce the approaching cars. The fare was ten cents. Organized in 1874 by David Butterfield and others, the

Below: Valley Street traffic from *Harper's New Monthly Magazine*, January, 1878. (Mary D. Hudgins Collection)

Above: City Post Office with mule-drawn trolley in foreground from *Frank Leslie's Illustrated Newspaper*, March 3, 1888. (Mary D. Hudgins Collection)

Below: Hot Springs Depot from *Hot Springs Illustrated Monthly*, 1879. (Walter Nunn Collection)

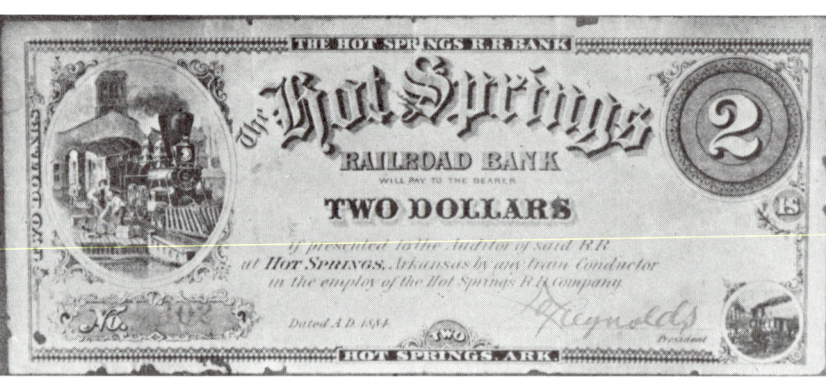

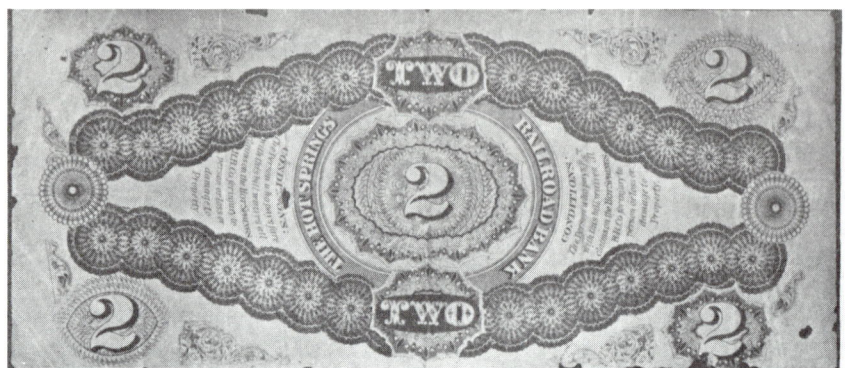

Above: Face (top) and back (bottom) of the pass issued by the Hot Springs R.R. Co., 1884 owned by James B. Dowds. (Mary D. Hudgins Collection)

Street Railroad Company paid the city an annual fee of ten dollars for each car in use on the line.

During Reynolds' first years of operating his narrow-gauge between Hot Springs and Malvern, it survived more than the usual number of difficulties facing railroads of that era. Because the cars were short and light of weight, they tended to derail frequently. Travelers accustomed to the comparative smoothness of standard-gauge cars complained about the quality of the ride. More and more passengers from distant cities also objected to leaving their comfortable Pullman cars before reaching their destination, but the Pullmans could not be switched to the Diamond Jo's narrow track. At last Reynolds realized that there was sufficient demand from the ever-increasing number of visitors for him to expend the necessary funds for widening his tracks to standard-gauge (four feet, 8½ inches). The work was completed in October 1889. For the first time Pullman cars with all their ornate 19th century magnificence could roll right into Hot Springs, bringing the *beau monde* of America, the rich and the famous, who could transform the town into the nation's smart watering place of the glittering 1890's, and on through the gaudy splendor of the *fin-de-siecle* into our own century.

Stephen Crane, who was then a free-lance writer for eastern newspapers, rode the Diamond Jo into Hot Springs in 1895. "As soon as the train reaches the great pine belt of Arkansas one becomes aware of the intoxication of the resinous air. It is heavy, fragrant with the odor from the vast pine tracts and its subtle influence contains a prophecy of the spirit of the little city afar in the hills. Tawny roads, the soil precisely the hue of a lion's mane, wander through the groves. Nearer the town a stream of water that looks like a million glasses of lemon phosphate brawls over the rocks.

"And then at last, at the railway station, comes that incoherent mass of stage drivers and baggagemen which badgers all resorts, roaring and gesticulating, as unintelligible always as a row of Homeric experts, while beyond them upon the sky are painted the calm turrets of the innumerable hotels and, still

Above: Signature of Diamond Jo Reynolds. (Mary D. Hudgins Collection)

Above: Valley Street showing the Hot Springs Hotel from *Harper's New Monthly Magazine*, January, 1878. (Mary D. Hudgins Collection)

Above: Cartoon of Samuel W. Fordyce, "a man of varied interests" from *Who's Who at Hot Springs*, 1905. (Mary D. Hudgins Collection)

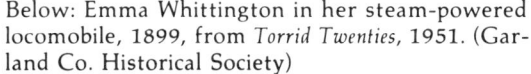

Below: Emma Whittington in her steam-powered locomobile, 1899, from *Torrid Twenties*, 1951. (Garland Co. Historical Society)

farther back, the green ridges and peaks of the hills. Not all travelers venture to storm that typical array of hackmen; some make a slinking detour and, coming out suddenly from behind the station, sail away with an air half relief, half guilt. At any rate, the stranger must circumnavigate these howling dervishes before he can gain his first glance of the vivid yellow sunlight, the green groves and the buildings of the springs."

Late in the 1890's the Diamond Jo lost its transportation monopoly. A promoter who bore the Dickensian name of Uriah Lott first attempted to build a railroad from Little Rock direct to Hot Springs and then on to Texas. When Lott's efforts failed in 1899, Colonel Samuel W. Fordyce took over, reorganized the company, and in one year brought the Little Rock & Hot Springs Western into town. Fordyce, a railroad man who had come to the Springs from Ohio in 1876, was almost as flamboyant a character as Jo Reynolds. He lent his expertise to development of the Hot Springs Street Railroad, built an elegant bath house, helped finance the Arlington Hotel, and became so enthusiastic a booster for his adopted home town that he invented legends to support his vision of the booming Spa's past. The town of Fordyce, seventy miles to the southeast, on the Cotton Belt Railroad which he built, was named for him.

Around the turn of the century, the Iron Mountain became the Missouri Pacific, and soon afterward absorbed the Hot Springs & Western into its lines. In 1902 the Diamond Jo also became a part of a giant system, joining the famed and late lamented Rock Island.

For a brief time Hot Springs was served by a third railroad, one that ran to the southwest and was developed out of a logging and sawmill line that was first known as Memphis, Paris & Gulf, and then Memphis, Dallas & Gulf. The M. D. & G., like many other ambitious short lines, could not meet its financial obligations, and it ceased operating after World War I.

By that time the automobile was coming into general use, the first one having appeared on the streets of the city in 1899. It was a steam-powered Locomobile, and fittingly its owner was Miss Emma Whittington, granddaughter of that forward-looking pioneer, Hiram Whittington.

The automobile, as we know now, eventually doomed the railroad passenger train, but without hard-surfaced all-weather roads, those early rubber-tired vehicles were scarcely more efficient than stagecoaches. Hot Springs waited a long time for paved roads, and even late into the 20th century lacked adequate highways. During the heyday of the Model-T, the Packard, and the Studebaker, motorists of the region somehow managed to reach the Springs over dusty or muddy roads, and then over gravel that flew through the air like buckshot behind every moving car so that windshields of the area appeared to have been webbed by malignant spiders. Visitors from afar continued to use the trains long after they had begun to vanish from other resorts, and then when acute deterioration of rail service set in, many switched to the airplane.

As early as the first decade of the century—while the Wright Brothers were perfecting their heavier-than-air flying machines—some citizens of Hot Springs turned their attention to lighter-than-air craft. Their interest may have been inspired by balloon ascensions at Whittington Park. At any rate, Joel T. Rice of the Royal community, a few miles west of town, designed a flying machine equipped with a gas bag. It was in effect a balloon that could be steered when aloft, somewhat like the dirigibles of Count Ferdinand von Zeppelin in Germany. In 1908, Rice persuaded Dr. W. H. Connell, S. J. Erickson, J. W. Westmoreland, and John A. Riggs, publisher of the *New Era*, to join him in forming the Hot Springs Airship Company. They named their first airship *Arkansas Traveler*, and Rice began constructing it on a vacant lot in the rear of the Garland County Courthouse.

Joel Rice's design included an undercarriage of steel to carry passengers, and it evidently was too heavy for the gas bag. On the morning of the first trial ascent, a crowd gathered behind the courthouse to watch the proceedings. When the ground lines were cut, the *Arkansas Traveler* lifted about twenty-five feet, and then floated slowly back to earth. After other trials failed, Rice transferred his efforts to the New York area, and although he succeeded in getting his airship aloft, it was accident-prone and could not compete with the rapid progress of the heavier-than-air machines. In 1910 he and his principal backer, John Riggs, were engaged in court suits which apparently ended the pioneer venture.

Failure did not long dampen local enthusiasm, however, for this exciting new way of bringing new visitors to the city. During the Arkansas State Fair of 1909, which was held in Hot Springs, the main feature of the event was the first airplane flight over the city. One newspaper described the plane as "a machine that does not have to depend upon a gas bag." In 1911 the Elks sponsored an aviation meet to which Glenn Curtiss brought his famous biplanes. They used the grass-carpeted infield of the Oaklawn Park race track for take-offs and landings. During the years following World War I, barnstorming veterans of the skies found Hot Springs to be particularly receptive to their visits. Tourists and citizens alike enjoyed exhibitions of stunt flying, and paid eagerly for short airplane rides over the green mountains.

In 1924 the Hot Springs Airport Company built a landing strip south of the city for the purpose of taking passengers for trips over the area. Within a short time visitors from distant places were using the runway to land their own or chartered planes. Thus was struck a second blow to the railroad passenger trains that had so long brought most visitors to the Spa. The future, it seemed, would soon belong to the air.

Below: John Riggs from *History of the Arkansas Press for 100 Years and More*, Fred W. Allsopp, 1922. (Walter Hussman)

Above: Advertisement for 1910 State Fair from *Arkansas Sketchbook*, 1910. (Garland Co. Historical Society)

CHAPTER III

THE AMERICAN SPA

"Here tottering forms,
but skin and bone,
Are rescued from the grave."

In 1818, Major Stephen H. Long reported that there were "sixty different springs or fountains of hot water, occupying a distance of about four hundred yards along the east side of the creek." In these springs (there are now forty-seven) flowing from the lower slope of the mountain named for them, was concentrated the future city's original reason for being. Without these waters, most likely a village to serve the inhabitants of the area would have arisen somewhere near the Ouachita River, certainly not in the present picturesque but improbable location. The young city had the shape of an elongated balloon squeezed tightly in the middle, its two parts connected by the narrow strait of Valley Street (Central Avenue) running between two mountains.

From the beginning of settlement, almost everyone who came and remained at the Springs had some sort of vision for the future that was linked to the wondrous waters. For that reason alone did visitors come there. The ailing came to ease distress, to bathe away their real or imagined pains. Scientists came from curiosity, to measure temperatures and analyze mineral content. An observation of 1878: "The hot waters rise to the surface through a formation of milk-white novaculite rock, on top of which they have deposited a layer of calcarious tufa, in some places of very considerable thickness."

Myriads of reports were published, listing the percentages or grains per gallon of magnesium, lime, iron, carbonic acid, alumina, potash, soda. Dozens of theories were advanced, none of which apparently had any great influence one way or the other upon the

Big Iron Spring. One gallon of water. Temperature, 148° Fahrenheit.

Lime	28.81
Magnesia	0.75
Alumina	5.14
Oxide of iron	1.16
Silicic acid	23.87
Carbonic acid	21.41
Sulphuric acid	4.43
Soda	1.49
Potash	2.05
Chlorine	0.75
Organic matter	8.46
Loss, etc.	1.68
Total	100.00

Above: Big Iron Spring and Professor J. W. Wardlaw's analysis of its water (1877) from *America's Baden-Baden Illustrated*, 1880. (Mary D. Hudgins Collection)

Below: Men enjoying the springs in the late 1800's. (Garland Co. Historical Society)

multitudes of bathers and imbibers who came each year in increasing numbers.

Privacy in which to bathe, a comfortable room for rest and sleep, a decent place to eat—these were the concomitant desires of every visitor. Remarkably these were met to some degree from the earliest years. First were the crude cabins and boarding house of John Percival and wife; then the Mellards' hotel built of logs in 1820, succeeded by the Beldings' more modern inn. In 1830 Asa Thompson built the first bath house, installing one wooden tub so that modest bathers willing to await their turns no longer had to seek privacy in wood thickets. Other bath houses soon followed.

One of the more enterprising persons to enter the field was John Cyrus Hale, who first came to the valley as a government surveyor in 1820, and then departed. A few years later he returned, and after buying Percival's pre-emption or squatter's rights,—which included the four hundred yards of thermal springs—he built the Hale Bath House and Hotel. Hale read the future correctly, but as we have seen, his claim was voided in the court decision of 1876. The Hale House nevertheless remained in business for many more years.

In the 1840's Hale formed a partnership with a Captain Haggerty of Cincinnati. Under the agreement Hale was to control the springs at the north end of the mountain while Haggerty managed those at the south end. When others attempted to move in on the territory, Hale was inclined to use force to drive them out. One violent incident occurring in July 1845 involved Thomas J. Reagan and "a big Missourian who was sojourning at the Springs." When Hale charged Reagan with violating his property rights, Reagan shot Hale. Hale's son then shot both Reagan and "the big Missourian." All recovered, and Hale held on to his claims.

In 1847 Hale enticed visitors to the springs with poems published as newspaper advertisements:

>Here nature calls from fortune's frown,
>   Her children of disease---
>And bids them throw their crutches down,
>   And go where'er they please . . .
>Let each come here, for here alone,
>   Exists the power to save;
>Here tottering forms, but skin and bone,
>   Are rescued from the grave.

Below: Old Hale Bath House built 1841. (Mary D. Hudgins Collection)

Above: Bird's-eye view of Hot Springs from *Harper's New Monthly Magazine*, January, 1878. (Mary D. Hudgins Collection)

Above: Photo by J. F. Kennedy of Rector Bath House, c. 1880. (Garland Co. Historical Society)

Inevitably, however, competitors attempted to share in Hale's monopoly. Jacob Mitchell took over a run-down hotel in 1846, improved its facilities, and advertised in New Orleans newspapers, emphasizing the tubs, spouts, and vapor baths available for the ailing. Henry M. Rector, the future governor, who had come to Hot Springs in 1843, challenged Hale's claim with a land grant he had inherited from his father Elias. Rector opened a tavern and bath house, advertising his establishment in distant newspapers and claiming that "the Hot Springs of Arkansas will renovate the most thread bare constitutions—set them up in a newness of life, Phoenix-like, and are unequaled by any desideratum in the known world."

In the 1850's the chief rival of Hale's establishments was Stidham's Hotel, which evidently was the successor to Rector's tavern, and was later advertised as the "Rector House." New bath houses were built near this tavern with "conveniences for warm-bathing for invalids." During the spring of 1854 forty-one people from Arkansas registered at Stidham's; thirty-four from Louisiana, thirty-three from Mississippi, fourteen from Tennessee, nine from Georgia, five from Kentucky, four from Missouri, two each from Texas, Alabama, Illinois, New York, Ohio and Virginia, and one each from Florida, Pennsylvania, South Carolina and Massachusetts. Two years later the preponderance of guests was reported to be from Pennsylvania, Missouri, Kentucky, Alabama, New York and the Creek Nation.

During the very decade that Hale and Thompson were making their first efforts to supply more pleasing accommodations for visitors, hydropathy or "the water cure" for human ailments was developing in Europe. Mineral springs soon became extremely popular with all classes of society. A small town bearing the name Spa in the Belgian Ardennes was the center for a therapeutic regimen based upon the drinking of and bathing in its waters. "Spa" eventually came to mean any locality containing a mineral spring resorted to for cures, and the name was applied to such fashionable places as Baden-Baden in Germany, Aix-les-Bains, France; Bath, England; White Sulphur Springs, Virginia; and somewhat belatedly, because of its remoteness, to Hot Springs in Arkansas.

"Not even Baden-Baden in Germany, nor any of the wells or springs of the old world or of the United States," wrote an anonymous sojourner at Hot Springs in 1873, "will be resorted to by a larger number of visitors." This same observer, who was from Georgia, told of how one might spend a morning visiting several springs that were then easily accessible, each one offering something unique. At the northern end of the slope and quite near Hot Springs Creek, which had not yet been covered, was Arsenic Springs, its waters issuing through a metal pipe. "This spring is much resorted to by the ladies," wrote the Georgian, "and it is often the case morning and evening, they may be seen congregated here quaffing the thermal water. It is said and generally believed by many of the fair ones, that this water has a tendency to heighten the complexion and beautify the skin." Whatever the merits of this spring, there was no arsenic in its waters.

Right: Cover to *America's Baden-Baden Illustrated* published 1880 by Iron Mountain R.R. Co. (Mary D. Hudgins Collection)

Below right: Arsenic Spring c. 1880 and an analysis of its water by Professor J. C. Wardlaw (1877). (Photo from Garland Co. Historical Society)

Below: Magnesia Spring from *Cutter's Guide to the Hot Springs of Arkansas,* 1882. (Mary D. Hudgins Collection)

"*Arsenic*" *Spring. One gallon of water.*
Temperature, 134° *Fahrenheit.*

Lime	30.60
Magnesia	4.57
Soda	1.79
Potash	1.94
Sulphuric acid	6.69
Silicic acid	23.36
Chlorine	1.67
Carbonic acid	22.38
Organic matter	5.12
Loss, etc.	1.88
Total	100.00

Below: The Egg Spring from *Hot Springs Illustrated Monthly*, February, 1878. (Garland Co. Historical Society)

Above: Alum Spring from *Hot Springs Illustrated Monthly*, 1879. (Walter Nunn Collection)

Right: "Corn Hole" from *Harper's New Monthly Magazine*, January, 1878. (Mary D. Hudgins Collection)

A few paces up the slope was Magnesia Spring. Although its flow of water, described as "crystal like," was channeled into the rear of the Rector House through tin tubing, those who wished to do so were welcome to take a seat in the hotel entry and drink as much as they liked. The Magnesia Springs water was a favorite of the Georgian, who said he preferred it to coffee or tea "when it can be had pure and hot, before the gases are allowed to escape."

Another popular spring was called the Sulphur and Iron. It was surrounded by an attractive growth of oak, pine, buckthorn and cedar. A quantity of egg shells was usually scattered around the four-foot square wooden curb that confined the bubbling water of the Sulphur and Iron, said to be hot enough to cook an egg in fifteen minutes. Nearby was Mud Springs, favored by sufferers from arthritis who took mud from its bottom and bound it to their ailing joints with cloths. Corn Hole Springs was popular with persons suffering from corns and other foot ailments.

Then there was the Pool of Bethesda, four yards square and about eighteen inches deep, with a few board seats around it. Some called it "old Ral," a play on the word "oldralgia" as opposed to "neuralgia." A visitor described the scene: "Here may be seen at all times of the day, but more especially morning and evening, the halt, the lame, the blind, some with contracted or crooked legs or arms, others with a stiff knee, ankle or arm, enlarged or swollen joints, neuralgia, gout, scrofulous taint or skin diseases, boils, tumors, and enlarged glands, old sores, syphilitic affections, etc... the white man and the colored man are often seen sitting together bathing their feet and legs, as everyone has undisputed right to bathe in this pool." There was also a Kidney Spring and a Liver Spring, said to be of great benefit to those who suffered from ailments of those bodily organs. "They call [it] Liver Spring," a sardonic New Yorker commented in 1876, "I suppose on account of the loose livers they find floating around it."

In the 1870's this was the outdoor scene all along that

Below: "Ladies' bath" c. 1860. (Arkansas History Commission)

Above: Women at the Corn Hole, c. 1874. (Garland Co. Historical Society)

Above: Water pipes from springs to bath houses as sketched by James. E. Taylor. Published in *Frank Leslie's Illustrated Newspaper*, October 25, 1873. (Mary D. Hudgins Collection)

Above: Boy with tin water pot from *Hot Springs, Arkansas, The Carlsbad of America*, 1893. (Hot Springs National Park)

invaluable four hundred yards of Hot Springs Mountain. Usually in the early mornings, vapor from the springs arose to envelop the vegetation and drift down over busy Valley Street below. In that decade Bath House Row was beginning to develop at the base of the springs where water could easily be piped into the buildings. Some houses, such as the Palace, Ozark and Magnesia, were built directly above the springs that furnished their water. The success of the original Hale and Rector bath houses rapidly encouraged many imitators. In addition some of the new hotels offered bathing facilities, notably the Hot Springs Hotel Bath House which advertised twenty tubs for men and four exclusively for ladies, at fifty cents per bath.

The routine of bathing indoors was somewhat improved over that of the ante-bellum days. The better houses had begun to employ attendants to assist the bathers, but the latter still were

Above: Arsenic Springs by J. F. Kennedy, 1874. (Arkansas History Commission)

Below: Big Iron Bath House from *Harper's New Monthly Magazine*, January 1878. (Mary D. Hudgins Collection)

Above: Valley Street with Arlington Hotel in left foreground c. 1880. (Mary D. Hudgins Collection)

expected to bring their own towels and blankets. This being the Victorian age when bathing *au naturel* was frowned upon, flannel underwear and a pair of heavy socks were also recommended. As the Spa custom of sipping hot mineral water while bathing in it had by this time been adopted from Europe, a special cup shaped like a coffee pot with a long nozzle to drink from was sold in stores along Valley Street (Central Avenue). The custom at most bath houses was to first register one's name on a slate and then await a turn at a tub. "It is often the case," observed a bather of the 1870's, "that some wily or wide awake watcher, is seen to steal a march on some of his neighbors, who are entitled to a bath before

Below: Palace Bath House from *Hot Springs Illustrated Monthly*, 1879. (Walter Nunn Collection)

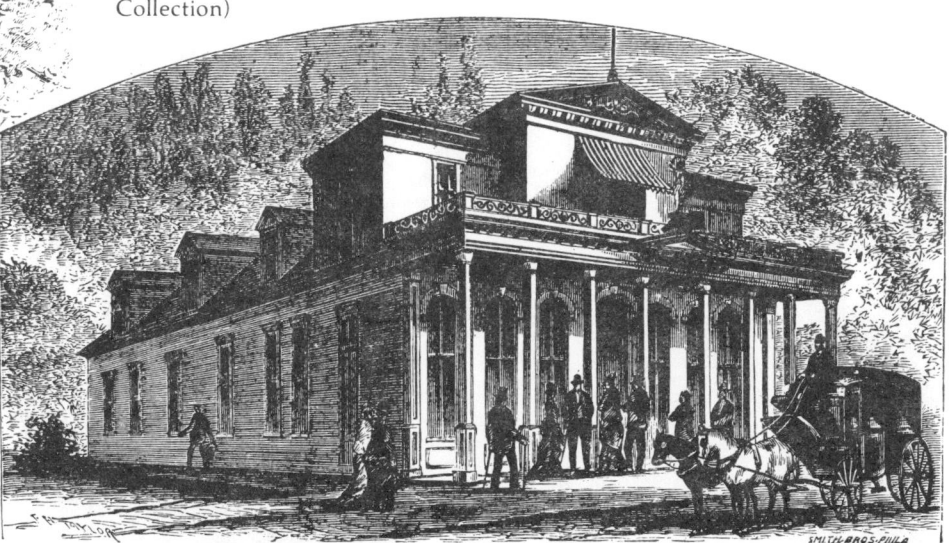

himself. This very often gets up a little quarrel, or sharp words between the parties; the proprietor's attention being called to the matter, he comes forward in most cases, [and] these little differences are settled in an amicable manner.

"Here we come to the bath rooms, together with the tubs which are in these most instances large and roomy, and are for the most part kept clean. We find a short bench which we take a seat on, while wall hooks are convenient to hang our dry goods on; we also find a thermometer and sand glass, the former being used to tell when your baths are too hot or too cold, while the latter is used to measure the time you should remain in the bath—It just requiring three minutes for this sand to run out . . . We find two faucets, one is used for letting in hot water, the other for what is called cold water, it having once been hot water, runs into vats where it is allowed to cool off. This is often above ninety-two degrees. It is drawn into the tub with the hot water; by this means one can temper the water . . . The baths usually recommended ranging from 90 to 100 degrees."

After relaxing for several minutes in a hot bath, the bather then went into a nearby vapor room to perspire profusely—much in the manner of the native Americans who had been taking such sweat baths for centuries. Steam rose through a lattice floor from vats filled with very hot water. The time spent here was determined by the bather, or his prescribing physician if he had one. Should no attendant be available, he rubbed himself down, wrapped in blankets, and made a dash for his hotel room. There he rested in bed for about half an hour and then dressed, ready to face the day in a glow of euphoria. There were surprises in store for some bathers, however, such as was reported by Frank Jebb of Batavia, New York, in March 1876: "Yesterday a lady who was taking a vapor bath discovered she was sitting on a snake. She managed to get out of the room and some men killed it—a large moccasin."

By the 1880's—a decade that Hot Springs historians call "the

Below: "Taking a bath" Park Hotel, from *Hot Springs, Arkansas, The Carlsbad of America*, 1893. (Hot Springs National Park)

Below: Bath house interior at the turn of the century. (Hot Springs National Park)

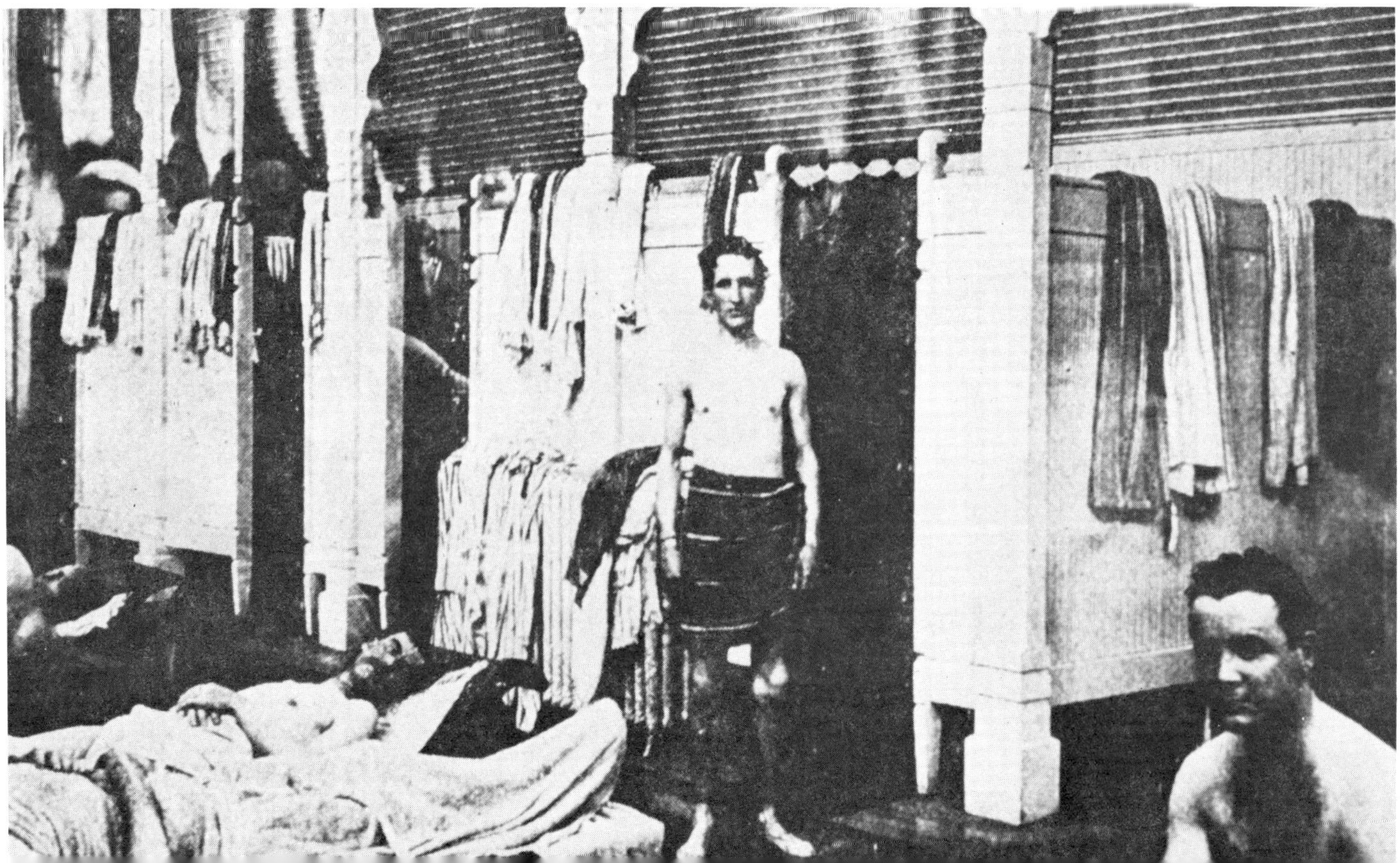

elegant eighties"—the Spa had won wide acceptance among the trend setters of America, travelers who were comparable to the "jet set" of today. In those days Florida was mostly a wasteland of sand and swamps, Las Vegas an empty desert, and California a continent away in train travel from the East. It became fashionable to visit the Springs for a series of baths regardless of whether one was ailing or not.

To meet the high standards of these *bon ton* visitors, more luxurious bathing facilities had to be provided. The Big Iron, for example, boasted of its speaking tubes and electrical annunciators. Most of the new houses replaced delapidated predecessors, or were built on what remained of leasable land along Bath House Row. Others were located on nearby city lots, or became extensions of hotels. The New Rector, Superior, Magnesia, Ozark and Lamar joined the Big Iron, Old Hale, Independent, Palace and Horseshoe on Bath House Row. The Buckstaff replaced the old Remmelsberg. Off the reservation, the Rockafellow, Hot Springs, Park, Alhambra and Eastman offered bathing equipment ranging from mediocre to sumptuous, and a number of hotels upgraded their bathing services.

Below: Quarterly report of government free bathing pools, giving number of baths, diseases treated and sexes of bathers ending November 30, 1885, from *Cutter's Guide to the Hot Springs of Arkansas*. (Mary D. Hudgins Collection)

Diseases of Bathers, Sex, etc.	Sept., 1885.	Oct., 1885.	Nov., 1885.	Total.
Number baths given ...	8386	6564	4893	19846
Rheumatism	3317	2613	1919	7849
Syphilis	2566	2001	1503	6070
General health	526	410	277	1213
Malaria	230	166	125	521
Paralysis	296	225	179	700
Sore eyes	141	110	87	338
Catarrh	205	161	125	491
Scrofula	178	140	104	422
Liver complaint	66	55	42	163
Erysipelas	22	18	13	53
Gonorrhœa	60	50	40	150
Kidney disease	55	45	36	136
Sciatica	43	35	27	105
Womb disease	104	81	62	247
Skin diseases	88	63	51	202
Nervousness	47	37	30	114
Locomotor ataxia	22	18	15	55
Ulcers	13	10	8	31
Dyspepsia	11	9	7	27
Eczema	58	45	33	136
Spinal affections	59	46	35	140
Stricture	57	45	36	138
Lupus	37	30	23	90
Measles	7	6	4	17
Neuralgia	152	123	95	370
Blood & lead poisoning	14	10	8	32
Hip disease	15	12	9	36
Males	6524	5095	4120	15739
Females	1865	1469	773	4107

Right: Cluster of bath houses from *Cutter's Guide to the Hot Springs of Arkansas*, 1887. (Mary D. Hudgins Collection)

A major obstacle to improving the decorousness of Bath House Row and the heart of the city was Hot Springs Creek, which from the beginning had served as a receptacle for the springs as it wound southward through the valley. With the increase in population during the 1870's, the creek became almost an open sewer. In dry seasons its current was sluggish and its odor offensive. Heavy rainstorms sometimes sent dangerous torrents racing down its rocky bed. To connect the two sides of Central Avenue narrow bridges were built along its sides to stop erosion, and cross-pole fences erected along the edges to prevent passersby from falling in after dark. Laundresses quickly discovered the fences were ideal for drying clothes, however, and this custom must have been an eyesore to visitors seeking aesthetic satisfaction along with physical relief.

A young New Yorker who accompanied his ailing mother to the Spa in 1876 was highly critical of the mile-and-a-half-long street. "When I add that there must be millions of pigs of all sizes and colors running at large, you can understand how pleasant pedestrianism must be. Hot Springs Creek runs along through the valley and crosses the road at least half a dozen times in a mile. As there are no bridges except foot bridges, of course those who drive enjoy frequent fording of the stream."

As a half mile of the creek ran through the federal reservation, the Department of the Interior was finally persuaded in 1884 to cover it with a masonry arch of sufficient dimensions to carry off any flood waters coming down from the hills. When this was completed the result was a 100-foot avenue through the heart of the growing city. Within a short time Central Avenue matched the fashionable spas of Europe in appearance. Neat rows of trees were planted along the street, with a paved sidewalk running beneath them. Fountains splashed on the grounds of hotels, and the architectural splendor of Bath House Row was admired by processions of strolling visitors.

"The motive of this main street is purely cosmopolitan," Stephen Crane observed in 1895. "It undoubtedly typifies the United States better than does any existing thoroughfare, for it resembles the North and the South, the East and the West. For a moment a row of little wooden stores will look exactly like a

Above: Hot Springs Creek near Arlington Hotel from *Harper's New Monthly Magazine*, January, 1878. (Mary D. Hudgins Collection)

Left: Hot Springs Creek 1883-1884 published by C.W. Calohan and Brother. (Garland Co. Historical Society)

Above: Hot Springs, showing principal street, bath houses, and Army and Navy Hospital from *Frank Leslie's Illustrated Newspaper*, March 31, 1888. (Mary D. Hudgins Collection)

portion of a small prairie village, but, later, one is confronted by a group of austere business blocks that are completely Eastern in expression. The street is bright at times with gaudy gypsy coloring; it is gray in places with dull and Puritanical hues. It is wealthy and poor; it is impertinent and courteous. It apparently comprehends all men and all moods and has little to say of itself. It is satisfied to exist without being defined or classified."

The author of *The Red Badge of Courage* was also impressed by the bath houses and the baths. The houses, he said, were close together and resembled mansions. "They seem to be the abodes of peculiarly subdued and home-loving millionaires . . . Crowds swarm in these baths. A man becomes a creature of three conditions. He is about to take a bath—he is taking a bath—he has taken a bath . . . In the quiet and intensely hot interiors of the buildings men involved in enormous bath robes lounge in great rocking chairs. In other rooms the Negro attendants scramble at the bidding of the bathers. Through the high windows the sunlight enters and pierces the curling masses of vapor which rise slowly in the heavy air."

Above: Ozark (top) and Rammelsberg (bottom) Bath Houses with newly planted trees c. 1885. (Garland Co. Historical Society)

Below: South end of bath-house row, 1884, from *Torrid Twenties*, 1951. (Garland Co. Historical Society)

But as Stephen Crane also observed, the Arkansas Spa welcomed the poor as well as the wealthy, the working class and the leisure class. In 1878, the first superintendent of the Hot Springs reservation, General Benjamin F. Kelley, noted that large numbers of indigent visitors were using one of the springs known as the "Mud Hole," also called the "Ral Hole," to bathe in. Although his orders were to drive all squatters and trespassers from federal property, he recognized that the unprosperous had as much right to benefit from thermal waters as did the prosperous, and he recommended that a wooden building be erected over Mud Hole. Known as the Free Bath House, it had no individual tubs but attracted so many users that in 1884 Kelley's successor, Colonel Samuel Hamblen, ordered it enlarged so that female bathers could

Above and Below: "Rhal City" c. 1877. (Garland Co. Historical Society)

NOTICE

All persons, either **residents or owners of temporary structures on the Hot Springs Reservation**, commonly designated as "**Rhal City**," or "**Hot Springs Mountain**," and all other shanties, tents or encampments within the limits of the reservation, are hereby required to remove the same within thirty days from this date.

Hereafter all persons are **forbid** erecting any building or **tent or** encamping on **this reservation.**

Hot Springs, Oct. 20, 1877.

**B. F. KELLEY,
Superintendent**

Above: "Rhal City" eviction notice. (Hot Springs National Park)

have a separate pool. By 1887, four hundred persons a day were going through the delapidated wooden building, and soon afterward it was torn down to be replaced by a masonry structure. Shortly after the turn of the century the Free Bath House was equipped with individual tubs, and from time to time through the years the government made additional improvements. In the 1920's the Park Service transferred jurisdiction to the Public Health Service. After World War II, the introduction of new "miracle drugs" diminished the popularity of spa therapy and led to a decline in use of the Free Bath House. It was closed in 1953, to be replaced by the modern Libbey Memorial Physical Medicine Center.

Above: The Mud Hole Bath House from *Hot Springs Illustrated Monthly*, 1879. (Walter Nunn Collection)

Right: The Mud Bath c. 1877, the first free bath house. (Garland Co. Historical Society)

Lower right: Exterior of Free Public Bath House, 1938. (Mary D. Hudgins Collection)

About the same time that the needs of impoverished health seekers were being recognized, several veterans of the Civil War decided that Hot Springs was the ideal place for a military hospital. Ever since the close of that deadly war, veterans from both sides had been coming to the springs to heal wounds and ailments acquired during their years of service. Many had insufficient funds to pay for medical treatment or private baths. Sympathetic to their plight was a fellow veteran, Dr. Algernon S. Garnett, a former Confederate surgeon who had been aboard the Merrimac when it engaged the Monitor—the world's first battle between ironclad ships.

With Colonel Samuel Fordyce and General John H. Logan (both former Yankee soldiers) Dr. Garnett formed an alliance to establish a military hospital at Hot Springs. General Logan had come to the Spa suffering from debilitating illnesses, and his recovery was so complete that he wanted other ailing veterans to benefit from the healing waters. Being a war hero, the founder of Memorial Day and a Senator from Illinois, "Black Jack" Logan had no difficulty in pushing a bill through Congress (June 30, 1882) establishing an Army and Navy Hospital.

Built on twenty-four acres of reservation land, the hospital was opened for use in January 1887. Through the years it served thousands of military personnel. By the late 1920's so many veterans of past wars were seeking admission that the Veterans Bureau and the War Department joined forces to fund the present magnificent structure. Completed in 1933, it proved to be a boon a decade later with the coming of World War II. In 1943, because of its heritage of water therapy, the Army and Navy Hospital became the official center for both rheumatism and polio. During the postwar period of economies and consolidations by the armed forces, proposals were made to close this historic institution. Eventually in 1959 the hospital's service to the military ended when it was converted to a civilian Rehabilitation Center.

When spa therapy reached its heady popularity during the last years of the 19th century a considerable number of unqualified and unscrupulous physicians swarmed into Hot Springs. To obtain patients in a hurry, they employed agents to board passenger trains at Little Rock or Malvern (and sometimes as far

Right: Drummer's license. (Mary D. Hudgins Collection, Archival Library, University of Arkansas at Fayetteville)

Below: Railroad Depot at Hot Springs where doctor's drummers awaited spa visitors from *Cutter's Guide to the Hot Springs of Arkansas*, 1884. (Mary D. Hudgins Collection)

Right: Army and Navy Hospital with Imperial Bath House in foreground, c. 1900. (Garland Co. Historical Society)

Below: Entrance to Army and Navy Hospital at the turn of the century. (Arkansas History Commission)

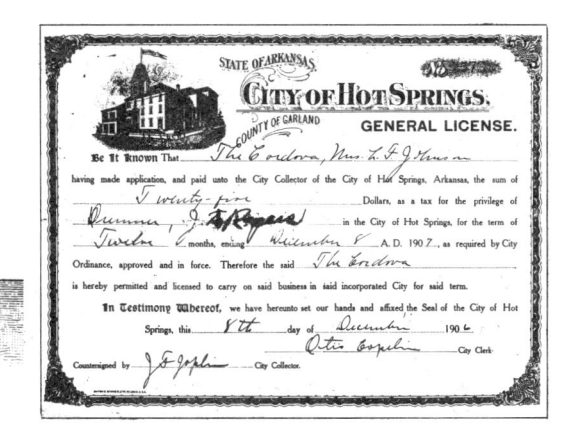

away as St. Louis) to meet incoming travelers and guide them to their offices. Known as "doctor drummers" or "doctor runners," the agents gradually widened their operations and income by adding hotels, boarding houses, bath houses and drugstores to their list of paying clients. As competition increased, the presence of "doctor drummers" on trains changed from a minor nuisance to a predatory horde, and so many visitors complained about them that the city council passed an ordinance declaring "drumming, running, or soliciting strangers or visitors" a misdemeanor within the city limits, subject to a fine of not less than ten dollars or more than twenty-five dollars.

As the law had no great effect outside Hot Springs and very little within the city, the council later decided to license the drummers, thus hopefully weeding out the worst of them. The new ordinance required agents to wear metal badges, and for a time this system eliminated some of the more serious abuses. But the drummers soon became so numerous at railroad stations they made it difficult for passengers to leave the cars. The drummers vied with each other, literally laying hands on disembarking passengers, offering free rides, medical treatments, and even meals.

In an effort to shield incoming visitors from the onslaught, the city had lines painted along the station platforms several yards from the rails, and ordered drummers to stand behind them. When this proved unenforceable, the drummers were ordered to keep off the platforms entirely, but their profusion of hacks, buggies and carriages continued to form a barrier for the harassed arrivals. "Here the scene is one of unparalleled confusion," a dismayed visitor said of the "perspiring, excited crowds of hotel, boarding house, and doctor's runners, hackmen and porters."

Eventually the power of the federal government had to be brought to bear upon "the drumming evil." Using the western cattlemen's stratagem of "cutting off the water," the reservation superintendent, Colonel William J. Little, warned that he would shut off use of the springs to any bath house or hotel that employed drummers. Little's successor, Martin Eisele, working with the city's mayors, tightened the rules still farther, and in 1904 President Theodore Roosevelt signed a regulation governing the conduct of Hot Springs physicians. Several doctors were indicted for using drummers, and some drummers themselves were brought into court. Gradually the obnoxious custom ended, but in a lively account of the phenomenon published in 1977, Hot Springs historian Mary D. Hudgins noted that the fight against doctor drumming had been so much a part of the city's life "that citizens even today scarcely dare recommend a single hotel or physician . . . in fear of being considered drummers."

Toward the end of the 19th century, the condition of many of the open springs began deteriorating at such a rate that successive reservation superintendents had to face the problem of preserving the hot water that was then so essential to the prosperity of the city. At first the sides of the springs were walled with bricks, and wooden roofs were built above them. Overuse by throngs of visitors, however, continued to threaten the water's purity. In the 1890's several of the larger springs were completely arched over, the hot water being piped into bath houses.

As some bath houses had been built directly above a spring, while other houses and hotels had to share in the limited general sources, disagreements and charges of monopoly began arising. In 1890, the federal government investigated the situation and found that the waters were unevenly distributed, some houses not receiving enough while others had so much they allowed it to be wasted. A recommendation to collect all the springs' waters into one central reservoir was bitterly opposed by the "haves," who claimed this would destroy the specific health values of the separate springs. Impartial scientists, however, soon disclosed what knowledgeable observers had suspected all along was a folk myth. Analysis proved that the waters of all the springs—Magnesia, Arsenic, Mud, Liver, Sulphur and Iron, and so on—were virtually the same in chemical content and radioactive properties, and that none alleviated any specific human affliction more than any other.

Consequently in 1891 efforts were started to collect the hot water from all the springs into a reservoir from where it could be fed to bath houses as it was needed. More than forty years passed, however, before the system was completed. After the National Parks Service was created in 1916, additional steps were taken to prevent pollution and insure preservation of the springs. And to provide modern visitors with an aura of what their antecedents experienced in the 19th century, two open springs were kept on display near the Promenade and are still there.

During the 1890's, as more and more springs were sealed with coverings, the successive superintendents noted that visitors were having difficulty finding hot water to fill their drinking cups and spouted cans. Colonel W. J. Little finally obtained funds for a drinking fountain, an elaborate marble creation that was named for John Noble, a Secretary of the Interior, and put into service near the Promenade in 1896. It is still in operation, near the entrance of the new Promenade on Reserve Street. In later years several additional fountains were placed at sites convenient for visitors. During the first half of the 20th century, among the most common sights in Hot Springs were lines of imbibers equipped with drinking cups awaiting their turns at fountains so that they might quaff the magic waters of the American Spa.

The opulent period of bath houses was yet to come, however. During the early years of this century and on through the roaring Twenties a spirit of elegance and luxury, reminiscent of old Rome at the height of its pagan glory, influenced the owners of the Spa's leading bath houses. They vied with each other in the acquisition of fancy accoutrements. They imported marble from Italy, installed colored glass windows, mosaics, and statuary, and employed thermal bathing experts from abroad. They remodeled

Above: Open display spring. (Hot Springs Chamber of Commerce)

Below: Arlington Spring covered. (Garland Co. Historical Society)

Below: John Noble drinking fountain c. 1900. (Garland Co. Historical Society)

Above: Ozark Bath House. (Mary D. Hudgins Collection)

Below: Men drinking at the Maurice Spring. (Hot Springs National Park)

Above: Middle of Bath-House Row at turn of the century with Horseshoe Bath House, Government Free Bath House and Magnesia Bath House in foreground. (Garland Co. Historical Society)

and rebuilt until Bath House Row took on the beauty that to this day impresses every passerby.

The domed, brown-tiled Quapaw replaced the Horseshoe and Magnesia. When the Buckstaff replaced the Rammelsburg, Corinthian columns were added to its front. Before the demise of the Imperial—across Reserve from the Hotel Eastman—the owners installed encaustic tiles and steel embossed ceilings. The Hale boasted of its 159 private sections, with cooling rooms, reading and writing rooms, massage and smoking rooms. The Maurice, rebuilt in 1912, featured Mott's Celebrated Victoria roll rim tubs, wicker couches for lounging, a gymnasium and sun parlor. F. F. Hellwig of Moscow, Russia, conducted electro-massage treatments while Mrs. Charlotte Hedwig of Sweden directed "original Swedish movements," all with "no muscle jerking or nerve-wracking sensations." The Ozark was proud of its Hitchcock Automatic Disinfecting Machines and offered "21 baths for 4 dollars."

Perhaps the most resplendent of all was Samuel Fordyce's noble structure, named for himself, that replaced the old Palace. Built of brick and terra cotta, with white stone framing the windows, it was done in Spanish Renaissance style. The marble interiors, stained glass, and enormous tubs gave it such an air of pomp and voluptuousness that bathers could easily imagine themselves in the Roman baths of Diocletian, with their perpetual streams of hot water pouring from founts with mouths of silver.

Someone, possibly Miss Alta Smith of the Chamber of Commerce, thought up the slogan "We Bathe the World," and indeed it seemed that way right up to the Depression years of the 1930's—to ebb and then resume on a less grand scale after World War II.

Below: 1930's convention badge designs. (Garland Co. Historical Society)

Above: "We Bathe The World" float for the centennial parade, 1936. (Mary D. Hudgins Collection)

CHAPTER IV
AMENITIES

"Most of the medical effects of Spa therapy are indirect, resulting from the relaxation of the patient as a result of the environmental factors of the Spa."

The environmental factors of the Spa—those were the dynamic elements that would keep Hot Springs flourishing whether the waters flowed or not, whether visitors chose to bathe in them or not. Even the most enthusiastic advocates of thermal treatments were aware from the earliest years that visitors seeking relaxation needed more than bath houses to fill their idle hours while taking the cure. The sturdier sojourners might go for bear and deer hunts in the nearby mountains, or angle for fish in the sparkling streams, or rent a livery stable horse for a ride into the countryside. But most of them wanted entertainment of the sort they could seldom find at home, and they were willing to pay for it.

After making a study of thermal treatments in the 20th century and questioning a number of authorities on the subject, Howard A. Rusk, a doctor specializing in rehabilitation medicine, reached this conclusion: "Most of the medical effects of Spa therapy are indirect, resulting from the relaxation of the patient as the result of the environmental factors of the Spa."

In that tranquil period before the Civil War, health seekers and citizens of the town commingled to entertain themselves with parties and balls and concerts and barbecues. "Much beauty and elegance," was the way the *Arkansas Gazette* of May 30, 1857, described the Hot Springs party dances held in hotel parlors. A few years earlier, however, the same newspaper reported that a proposed convalescents' ball had been vetoed "by the cripples, as their dancing would prove a *lame* affair."

Above: Castle Park from *America's Baden-Baden Illustrated*, 1880. (Mary D. Hudgins Collection)

Below: Turn-of-the-century picnic. (Garland Co. Historical Society)

The first commercial theatrical performance may have been a concert given on May 20, 1856 by "the Blind Vocalists," a popular quartet of that time. Three years later, in the spring of 1859, a small theater was built at the Spa, and an actors' stock company arrived soon afterward. Their reception must have been enthusiastic because they remained for much of the season, adding other members, including "a jig dancer and Ethiopian delineator." A newspaper boasted that Hot Springs was the "only watering place in the South, if not the whole country, which affords theatrical amusements to its visitors."

A few months later, however, this glorious promise for the future vanished under the storm of civil war. Afterwards in the years of struggling to be reborn, the town offered little in the way of theatrical entertainment until the late 1870's, and it was not until the beginning of the "Elegant Eighties" that big-time theater came to Hot Springs.

The peripatetic railroad builder and financier, Samuel W. Fordyce, who had "adopted" Hot Springs for his home town, was a leading mover behind construction of an ornate Victorian-style Opera House at 200 Central Avenue. On October 6, 1882, workmen completed installation of its galvanized iron front, and on November 20, the play *Virginius* opened with Frederick Warde in the leading role.

As was the case with most other "opera houses" of that era in America, very few grand operas were performed on the Hot Springs stage. But because of guaranteed audiences willing to pay for the best entertainment, as well as the quality of the building itself, Central Avenue's Opera House was soon receiving plays direct from New York, performed by the leading actors of the day.

Below: Opera House bill, 1883. (Mary D. Hudgins Collection)

Above: Fishing at Thornton's Mill, the falls of the Ouachita River from *Hot Springs Illustrated Monthly*, 1879. (Walter Nunn Collection)

Above: Turn of the century carriage ride on Hot Springs Mountain. (Garland Co. Historical Society)

Furnished with red velvet seats, carpets and tapestries, the theater also boasted a dress circle and four boxes. The stage was equipped with trap doors and skids for rapid changes of scenery. Among the Opera House's unique features were the exits which required no stairways even for the balcony, but led directly out upon the side of West Mountain. On opening nights of such classical dramas as *Rip Van Winkle*, with the great Joseph Jefferson, audiences would arrive in their carriages wearing full dress. For these occasions even the ushers were required to wear tuxedos. After the first performance, it was not uncommon for some of the leading families of the city to hold receptions for the cast.

When performers with mass appeal came to town—such as Phineas Barnum's midget, General Tom Thumb—parades were staged along Central Avenue so that all could see the celebrities of the day. Among the famous actors and actresses who starred on the Opera House stage were Lillian Russell, John Drew, Billie Burke, James O'Neill (father of playwright Eugene O'Neill) and Evelyn Nesbit, who was known as "the girl in the red velvet swing" after her husband, Harry K. Thaw, shot and killed architect Stanford White in what was described as a "fit of jealous rage." *Floradora*, a musical with a cast of one hundred, including Evelyn Nesbit, outdrew O'Neill's *Count of Monte Cristo* by four to one. Other presentations that were popular enough to be repeated each season included David Belasco's *Zaza*, *Captain Jinks of the Horse Marines*, *Ten Nights in a Bar Room*, *Sherlock Holmes*, *Way Down East*, and *Uncle Tom's Cabin* with a "pack of genuine bloodhounds from Tennessee." *The Wizard of Oz* was as popular in 1904 as it is now. The plays of Ibsen and Shakespeare drew sizable audiences, and occasionally a genuine opera company presented selections. Minstrel shows, however, were probably the most popular musical attractions, with their lively tunes, dancing, and comedy sketches.

Below: Hot Springs Opera House. (Garland Co. Historical Society)

One problem was obtaining enough first-rate productions to supply the constant demand from both citizens and visitors for stage entertainment. In 1899 an energetic young man named Frank Head arrived from Illinois to take over management of the Opera House. He set out to keep the stage lighted every night, bringing in concert groups, lecturers, boxing matches and vaudeville acts when plays were unobtainable. For some reason, vaudeville never caught on with the audiences who attended the Opera House. "Vaudeville seems to be a failure in this city," *Billboard Magazine* reported March 17, 1906. "Theater goers are patiently awaiting the coming of Dockstader's Minstrels."

Around the turn of the century, after providing entertainment for a generation of theater goers, the Opera House began showing signs of deterioration. Tastes were also changing. Productions fresh from Broadway required larger stages for their presentation and larger audiences to cover their costs. And that new invention, the motion picture, was making its entrance upon the scene.

In 1903, Manager Frank Head accepted an offer from the city for use of a site on Benton Street to construct a new theater to be known as the Auditorium. It opened on March 8, 1904, with a performance by the famed coloratura, Adelina Patti, on her farewell tour. The new theater's stage was said to be the second largest in the South, more than adequate for a large treadmill necessary for presentation of the popular *Ben Hur*. For a few more years the declining Opera House continued with sporadic offerings but during the first World War it closed, and after forty years of neglect the grand old building met the fate of many memorable American architectural landmarks—it was demolished to provide space for parking automobiles.

The Auditorium meanwhile provided the best of America's stage entertainment enacted by performers whose faces would soon be appearing on motion picture screens. In 1910, Frank Head himself recognized the inevitable and joined with others in building the Princess Theater for motion pictures. About the same time Sidney Nutt converted the Central Theater to movies, and later took over management of the Princess. During the golden years of the silver screen, when Hollywood was producing hundreds of films each year, several other theaters were built, each passing through the era of mammoth pipe organs to sound pictures, followed by out-of-door drive-ins and then the decline of

Above: Frank Head. (Mary D. Hudgins Collection)

Below: Handbill for Jeffries-Johnson fight pictures at the Auditorium Theater. (Mary D. Hudgins Collection)

Below: City Hall and Auditorium Theater with special theater entrance on the side. (Mary D. Hudgins Collection)

JEFFRIES-JOHNSON FIGHT PICTURES

COME ON BOYS!
The Season's Sporting Event

TRUE AS LIFE
From the RINGSIDE to YOUR CITY.

15-Rounds-15

Positively the Original Pictures.

DON'T MISS IT!

Right: Princess Theatre at night from *Night in Hot Springs*, 1912. (Mary D. Hudgins Collection)

Right: Arlington Hotel draped for Robinson's vice-presidential notification, KTHS broadcast tower on roof. (Garland Co. Historical Society)

Above: Sidney M. Nutt. (Garland Co. Historical Society)

movie-going in our own era.

With the advent of the electronic age, few live acts were available for the stage of the Auditorium Theater. Its management turned to prize fights and wrestling matches and eventually in 1962 the building was replaced by the present City Hall and Auditorium. In the 1970's, out-of-door live drama was attempted with *The Conquistadors*. Based on the legend of De Soto's visit to the area in 1541, it was designed to be repeated each season but failed to attract sufficient audiences to meet the cost of production.

In 1924 the Arlington Hotel brought radio to Hot Springs. Using the call letters KTHS, or "Kum to Hot Springs," the first broadcast reached at least twenty-three states. After the station's power was increased and it received a clear channel license in 1928, the signal could be heard across the continent. When Arkansas's Senator Joseph T. Robinson started his vice-presidential campaign as a running mate to Al Smith, he made his first broadcast from the Hot Springs station. *Lum and Abner*, one of the most popular radio shows of the period, also started here. In 1961, KFOY—TV (Channel 9) sent the first television signals from its tower on West Mountain. Largely as the result of the compression of time and space resulting from advanced telecommunications, and the modern trend toward concentration of resources, the legendary KTHS and Channel 9 both went elsewhere. Other radio stations, however, continue to provide Hot Springs with local programming.

Gambling—the word comes from the Old English *gamen*, or game. It is as ancient as the language, and through the centuries gambling meant to play, to disport oneself. Somewhere along the way, the players added risk and suspense to games by wagering something of value, and as has happened to many words, the meaning of gambling changed. Gambling is still play, but the word carries a pejorative burden—like the word glutton which originally meant simply to swallow, but was changed in meaning by those who swallowed too much.

Being a city where people come to play and disport themselves, gambling in one form or another has been a natural part of the amenities at Hot Springs at least as far back as 1849 when a correspondent for *The Spirit of the Times* reported: "There are two billiard tables here. Each do a pretty good business during the day, and at night they play Rondo." Bets on this old French game were decided by the number of odd or even balls that remained on the table after they were pushed from one corner of the table to the opposite. The bets in Hot Springs ran as high as five dollars, easily equal to about fifty now.

In the summer of 1873 a visitor noticed upon a building on Valley Street a large sign: HOLE IN THE WALL. "We have been informed," he said. "by a western Texian (who no doubt knows whether there was a hole in the wall or not) that the more one laid down the less he had to pick up; we are not familiar enough with this business (gambling) to give you names of the different games indulged in here for money, but would suppose the list to comprise all the games known in larger cities."

Only a decade later a newspaper correspondent reported that gambling was a recognized institution at the Spa "and does not hide its head in by-ways as it does 'up among the Yanks.'" He added: "Gamblers occupy an anomalous position at Hot Springs. They may be said to have discovered the place, as they and Mississippi River men were the first to come and profit by the 'waters of life.' They are always here in great force. Indeed, it is difficult to find a gambler in any large city, North or South, who does not know the place and all about it."

In that year, 1884, gambling had grown so profitable for operators of gaming establishments that they split into two factions, one led by Frank Flynn, the other by Major S. A. Doran. Flynn was a Canadian who visited the Springs during the renaissance following the Civil War, and like many others decided to remain. He was a slight man with delicate features, thinning black hair, and jet black eyes "that remain still for an instant, but wander all around the room as if in search of something." Through the years he somehow gained sufficient power over the local gambling element to be known as "Boss Gambler." By 1884 six or seven houses on Central Avenue dominated the business—the Arlington, Billy McTague's, the Owl, the Ozark Club, the Palace, Monarch, and Office, the last of which was Flynn's headquarters. For all of them the architectural style was virtually the same, two floors with a saloon on the street level and gambling rooms upstairs.

Flynn controlled or exacted tribute from all the first-class places except the Palace and Monarch which were owned by Jim Lane, a "sporting man" from Cairo, Illinois. As early as 1881, Flynn made attempts to bring Lane under his dominance but the latter rebuffed all overtures and threats until one night when Flynn and a mob of bully boys invaded the Palace. They destroyed all the equipment, overturned tables or tossed them out windows, and frightened all the customers away. Although Lane's dealers resisted and managed to kill one of Flynn's men in the brawl, Lane himself was so shaken by the assault that he left town in fear of his life.

During the months that followed, Lane crossed paths with

Above: Card game at a mountain camp from *America's Baden-Baden Illustrated*, 1880. (Mary D. Hudgins Collection)

Below: Valley Street from *Hot Springs Illustrated Monthly*, 1879. (Walter Nunn Collection)

Major S. A. Doran, probably in New Orleans. Doran was a formidable figure. His six-foot three, 220-pound body moved with the military bearing acquired during his Confederate Army service. His voice was gruff but usually friendly. When he learned of Lane's troubles with Flynn, he resolved to challenge the "Boss Gambler" in his own territory. Sometime earlier Doran evidently had met Flynn in the gambling houses of Austin, Texas, and did not care for him.

Early in the winter season of 1883-84, Major Doran arrived in Hot Springs and quietly began refurbishing Lane's closed Palace. By this time Flynn had become more arrogant than ever. According to "Omaha Frank" Borland, a part-time gambler and dealer, Flynn disliked for his customers—especially Texans—to quit a game when they were too far ahead. Borland told of an incident in which a visiting Texan left a seven-up game with a pocketful of the Office gambling establishment's money. "Young man," Flynn warned him, "you haven't won enough to pay your fine for gambling." The Texan laughed, walked out on the street and a few minutes later was arrested on Flynn's order and fined heavily for illegal gambling.

Although Flynn made several efforts to force Doran into his so-called "ring," the major went blithely ahead with plans to operate independently. Flynn then secretly began recruiting gunmen from Texas and the Territories farther west. In addition he used his two brothers, Jack and Billy, as bodyguards. When Doran learned of this, he brought in some gunfighter friends of his own. They included Bob and Dave Pruitt, Harry Lansing, Ed Howell, John Allison, and Jake Lucius, a half-blood from the Indian Nation. Lucius was the most professional in appearance, being mild-mannered, tall, lank, and copper-skinned, with coal-black eyes always alert, and he usually wore a cowboy Stetson. With two gathering armies of quick-draw artists, Hot Springs began taking on the atmosphere of such places as Dodge City, Kansas, or Tombstone, Arizona.

Early in February, Major Doran announced a grand opening, invited the leading citizens of Hot Springs and hired a brass band to play through the evening in front of the Palace. A newspaper correspondent reported the affair: "Upstairs the two handsomely furnished rooms were thronged with lawyers, doctors, bankers, the most respectable citizens of the place, crowded around faro or stud-horse poker games, or at the supper tables groaning under gigantic pyramids of chicken-salad and sandwitches; whiskey and champagne flowed like water. The rough element was there, too, but on its best behavior, for scattered about the rooms were 'the Major' and his satellites, 'well-heeled' and ready for action."

With so many leading citizens present, Major Doran must have been fairly confident that Flynn would not try anything violent on opening night. After that first lively evening, however, patronage fell off sharply, not only in the Palace but in all the gambling establishments. Each side appeared to be waiting for the other to attack, and like two belligerent nations, each tried to outdo the other in armaments. In the Palace, Dave and Bob Pruitt kept their Winchester rifles beside their faro tables, and the other dealers were similarly prepared. Three days passed, and then on the morning of the fourth, one of the town's veteran gamblers, a man named Tom Dale, entered the Palace and called Doran aside. While they talked quietly for a few moments Doran lit a cigar, and then he followed Dale downstairs and out upon Central Avenue.

Conflicting accounts were told of what happened next. "Omaha Frank" Borland, who was playing poker in the Palace at the time, later said that about ten or fifteen minutes passed before shots were fired, and that shortly afterward Major Doran reappeared at the head of the stairs, his half-smoked cigar still clamped between his teeth. According to Borland, Dale had brought Doran a message from Flynn challenging him to come out and meet him for a shoot-out in the street, Old West style. Doran sighted Flynn on a street corner, warned him to draw, and both men began firing. The duel was a fiasco, more or less. Doran's first shot misfired. He tossed the pistol aside and drew another, while Flynn fired and missed his target. With a long-barreled revolver, Doran hit Flynn in the chest, causing him to stagger back into a doorway. Thereupon Doran holstered his six-gun and returned to the Palace, where he complained that his challenger had been wearing a coat of mail. "I know I hit him once over the heart," he said. "I saw the dust fly off his coat. Next time I hit him I'll plug him in the eye."

Flynn evidently had been only slightly wounded, but his supporters claimed that Doran's attack upon him had come without warning. Flynn, they said, was wearing a buttoned overcoat, not a coat of mail, and Doran had not given him time to draw his weapon. Popular opinion in Hot Springs had favored Flynn all along; the "Boss Gambler" might be a rascal, but he was a local rascal, known to everyone in town, while Doran was still the outsider.

This attitude was quickly reversed, however, after it was learned that Flynn's next move was to rent a room in the Arlington Hotel with a window overlooking the entrance to the Palace. Flynn and some of his hirelings, armed with rifles and shotguns, kept a constant watch from this ambush position, intending to gun down Doran when he was leaving or entering the Palace. Rumors of the ambush leaked out to such an extent that a small group of the curious frequented the balcony of Billy McTague's saloon for a close-up view of the shooting, if and when it occurred.

To the sporting crowd, Flynn's ambush was unsporting, to say the least, and the town's sympathies shifted toward Doran. As for Doran, the hotel-room snipers must have been the last straw. He evidently decided that he would have to destroy Flynn and his gunmen before they destroyed him.

The showdown on Central Avenue was a precursive model for the bootlegger battles on the streets of Chicago forty years later. On visits to Hot Springs in the 1920's, Chicago's most famous son, Al Capone, may have heard about the Flynn-Doran battle. In 1884, however, instead of an automobile the vehicle was a horse-drawn cab, and instead of Tommy-guns the weapons were western-style six-shooters.

On one of those infrequent but gloomy drizzly mornings that come to Hot Springs in mid-winter, Frank Flynn and his two brothers, Jack and Billy, were riding in a cab near the south end of Bath House Row. Seven or eight of Doran's gunmen were posted nearby along the plank sidewalks or in doorways. Suddenly shooting started, and in the first wild volley Jack Flynn was mortally wounded and the cab driver was shot dead from his box into the street. When Frank and Billy Flynn leaped out to return fire, both were hit in a second round of bullets. Meanwhile the frightened horses, dragging their reins, galloped away with the now empty vehicle.

Billy made his way to the sidewalk in front of the two-story Visitors' Home opposite the Rammelsburg Bath House. One witness reported seeing Frank armed with a Winchester rifle in the entrance of the Ozark Saloon near Court Street. Another said he took refuge in the lobby of the Hot Springs National Bank where a doctor came to dress his wounds.

By this time the Chief of Police, Tom Toler, had reached the scene and was attempting to disperse the crowd. Other casualties were now being found, victims of the inevitable stray bullets that fly during street battles. The driver of a dray cart was killed outright while seated on his vehicle, and a man standing in the doorway of a barber shop was severely wounded.

While the police were clearing the street, the town's firebell

Above: Central Ave. looking south during the era of the Flynn-Doran showdown, from *Hot Springs Illustrated Monthly*, 1879. Arlington Hotel is the three-story structure in the left foreground. The Palace was across the street. (Walter Nunn Collection)

which was used for all emergencies began an insistent clanging. As both factions of professional gamblers were to learn later, this was a signal for a gathering of responsible citizens. A few days earlier, after the first shootout between Flynn and Doran, the townspeople who opposed violence had organized a Committee of Twelve to put a stop to it. They were concerned not only for the safety of the community but for the growing image of danger that would frighten away health seekers. Within a matter of minutes after the shootout on Central Avenue—which had left three people dead in the street—the Committee decided that gambling as practiced in Hot Springs had ceased to be an amenity that would bring pleasure to visitors. The members solemnly pledged themselves to drive every gambler associated with Flynn or Doran out of the city and county.

During the next several days the Committee of Twelve did exactly that. Lists of gamblers' names were drawn up, and one by one they were presented with notices giving them twenty-four hours to leave the Spa. If they failed to obey, the Committee armed with bayonetted rifles went to their living quarters, packed their belongings, escorted them to the Diamond Jo railroad station, and bought each one a ticket to Malvern. Frank Flynn, it was said, stood on the platform of the outgoing train, shaking his fist at members of the Committee and shouting unprintable words. One of the correlative acts of the reformers was a raid on the office of a newspaper, *The Horseshoe*, which had been linked to Flynn's activities. Because the editor refused to leave town promptly, the Committee destroyed his printing equipment with sledge

Below: Billy Flynn. (Ann Dunbar, Dallas, Texas)

Below: Frank Flynn. (Ann Dunbar, Dallas, Texas)

hammers, effectively putting him out of business. Major Doran apparently left Hot Springs without resistance, transferring his activities to Fort Smith. There a few years later, he was killed by a man who had quarreled with him over a woman.

In Hot Springs, as soon as the last of the gamblers associated with Flynn or Doran were banished from the city, the clubrooms were permitted to open once again. Officials of both the city and the county imposed taxes on the establishments that were probably less than the payoffs formerly exacted by the "Boss Gambler." The officials also let it be known that any gambler caught running a dishonest game or cheating in any way would be heavily fined and ordered out of town. Once again gambling was restored as a proper amenity of the American Spa.

And so in the decade of the "elegant Eighties" was established the pattern that the people of Hot Springs would follow for many years in their ambivalent attitude toward casino gambling. Some were utterly opposed to the practice, some tolerated it, some favored it heartily. Yet almost all would join ranks whenever the pendulum swung too far toward corruption and violence. When this happened they turned against those who lost their sense of moderation and gluttonlike tried to swallow too much.

For long periods of time after Flynn-Doran, gambling at Hot Springs served as a convenient "black beast" for state politicians who needed something to rail against, or to tar their opponents with. Early in the 20th century, Jeff Davis in his races for governor and U.S. Senator, found it most useful, and so did others to a lesser degree. Whenever needed to help a state politician get elected, or to help keep him in office, the illegal casinos were usually accommodating enough to close down for whatever length of time was deemed appropriate.

Below: World War II veterans sworn into county offices, (left to right) E.M. "Buddy" Houpt, I.G. Brown, Clyde H. Brown, Sid McMath, Leonard Ellis, Jo Campbell, Ray Owen, and Q. Byrum Hurst. (Sid McMath)

Above: Leo Patrick McLaughlin. (Garland Co. Historical Society)

Below: The Vapors. (Mark Palmer Collection)

The next big showdown brought on by gambling forces occurred in 1946, when returning veterans of World War II took on the colorful boss mayor, Leo Patrick McLaughlin. For years McLaughlin had dominated the gambling interests somewhat in the same way that Frank Flynn had done in the 1880's. It was McLaughlin's stranglehold on politics that infuriated the young World War II veterans. Led by Sidney McMath they went after McLaughlin with such energy that his power was demolished and he was brought to trial on charges of bribery and malfeasance. "Garland County Cleansed of Sin," was the way one magazine writer described the event. McLaughlin survived two long trials, however, and was never convicted, living on in the town he no longer controlled until he died in 1958.

McLaughlin's departure from the scene ended open gambling for a time, but the vacuum was soon filled by others, who were said to be controlled by "the mob" or other mysterious outside forces. Vincent Owen Madden, a well-known figure in organized crime in New York, had come to the Spa in 1930. His life in Hot Springs was surrounded by rumors and conjectures. Outwardly he was a model citizen, but the public believed he he was the real "Boss Gambler" behind the jaunty front of Mayor McLaughlin. (The entire mid-20th century era of gambling at Hot Springs is an undocumented story that would require months of research to reconstruct, including carefully cross-checked personal interviews and intensive examination of federal and state records that are only now being made available for public use.)

During the summer of 1959, Dane Harris, a prominent local gambler, built the Vapors supper club and rapidly became a big name in town. According to a correspondent for the *Saturday Evening Post*, Harris joined the Chamber of Commerce, contributed to all church fund drives, and gave the city two swimming pools— one for whites and one for blacks. Apparently he also had close connections with Owen Madden.

Late in 1961, Congress passed a federal anti-gambling law to aid local officials in enforcement. Discovering that illegal gambling had flourished in Hot Springs for years, the Department of Justice summoned Owen Madden and mobster Joseph Valachi, among others, for questioning. Madden communicated very little; Valachi said that because of its waters Hot Springs was a popular "gathering spot for New York and Chicago hoodlums." The Justice Department reached the conclusion that Hot Springs had "the largest illegal gambling operation in any state," and that neither the state nor local government was doing anything about it. Consequently a grand jury met at Fort Smith to examine the situation from a reasonable distance, but after considerable deliberation found no violation of federal laws.

When an out-of-state reporter asked Dane Harris how illegal gambling could continue to flourish with such impunity, Harris replied: "There is no reform group. There never has been. We are respected; there's no feeling that we're doing something unlawful."

Reform groups did exist, however, and in 1964 allied themselves with Winthrop Rockefeller in his race for governor against Orval Faubus. "Just because there's been gambling here for a hundred years doesn't make it right," said one aggrieved resident of Hot Springs. "They've been robbing banks a long time too." Governor Faubus, who had done nothing to disturb Hot Springs gambling during his decade of tenure in office, suspected that Rockefeller might defeat him with votes of the anti-gambling electorate around the state. During the preceding months gambling and prostitution had become more blatant than ever in Hot Springs. A falling out among the gambling elements also had led to violence. Bombs were set off in the Vapors restaurant and casino and at the homes of those involved. Madam Maxine Harris, adopting the advertising method of the Ostrich Farm, which trotted its big birds down Central Avenue, occasionally loaded her prettiest girls into a red and white Ford convertible and with the top down drove them along the Avenue, displaying samples of the wares offered at her Palm Street "mansion."

Responding to the situation with his usual political sagacity, Governor Faubus ordered the doors of the Hot Springs casinos closed. A group of legislators tried to halt the move by introducing

Right: Central Avenue night life, 1950's. (Hot Springs Chamber of Commerce)

Below: Exterior, Southern Club at night. (Mark Palmer Collection)

Below: Gambling at the Tower Club, January, 1956. (Arkansas History Commission)

Above: Exterior, Belvedere Club. (Mark Palmer Collection)

Above: Interior, Belvedere Club. (Hot Springs Chamber of Commerce)

a bill to make gambling legal, but it failed. March 29, 1964, was the night the money stopped. Xavier Cugat and Abbe Lane were performing at the Belvedere, but the usual gaiety was missing from the popular club. "The wolf's in the woods and there's no use making out he's not," was the comment of one casino operator. However, a knowledgeable city official was less worried: "We'll be open this time next year," he assured an inquiring reporter.

Within days seven large conventions were canceled, and the owners of the Vapors, Belvedere and Southern clubs were desperately seeking ways of getting their craps tables going again "before everyone starves to death for lack of hundred dollar bills."

Philip Hamburger, a writer for the *New Yorker*, found a number of disappointed out-of-town visitors still hopeful that gambling would soon resume. One of them told Hamburger that while taking a steam bath he'd had a vision of a floor show in the Vapors Club, "with people eating immense steaks while Mickey Rooney told jokes up on the stage and imitated Jimmy Stewart. I could hear people gambling in the next room, and I could see in my mind's eye the big doors swinging open to the gambling room and to the muted but hysterical hum of voices and the click of the machines and the strange-looking women betting like fiends, with their crazy blond hair and purple hair and green hair."

But during the Faubus-Rockefeller campaign of 1964, the vision remained only a vision. Most of the out-of-town observers departed, the *Saturday Evening Post's* man firing a final shot at the "unrepentant little resort . . . fighting for its low, evil, up-all-night, bad-example-setting and extremely comfortable life."

However, it was a short dry spell for the gamblers at the Spa. Faubus overcame the first Rockefeller challenge, and machines were soon clicking again in the gambling rooms of the big clubs.

Two years later Winthrop Rockefeller was back in contention, but this time Faubus did not choose to run, and Rockefeller defeated the Democratic candidate, Justice Jim Johnson. Early in 1967, after he took over the governorship, Rockefeller began quietly putting pressure on Hot Springs law enforcement officials to close down illegal gambling. When little was done by the locals, the new director of state police, Lynn A. Davis, started a series of raids against the casinos, seizing hundreds of slot machines and other gambling paraphernalia. At first the devices were turned over to the Hot Springs police for possible prosecutions but when Davis discovered that many of the machines were being returned to casinos, the state police began breaking them up first. The resourceful gambling fraternity succeeded in recovering the broken machines, however, and subsidized a number of repair shops. The state police retaliated by raiding the repair shops, and on one occasion found a large cache of machines in a parked truck.

Evidence that the casino operators were becoming excessive in their greed was discovered during the raids. Many of the craps tables were outfitted with "juice joints," devices fastened beneath the tables and hooked to batteries so that the croupiers could determine the final positions of thrown dice.

On the night of October 7, 1967, Colonel Davis and the state police made one of their most damaging raids. After obtaining a search and seizure warrant from a cooperative municipal judge, Davis visited the residence of Harry Columbus, manager of the Southern Club, and behind his home was a large storehouse, its solid door padlocked. When Davis asked Columbus for the key, the club owner refused to comply, whereupon the police broke the door down. Inside they found two truckloads of slot machines labeled with such club names as Ramada, Whispering Winds, Chick Inn and Red Barn. Fifteen of the machines had markings the state police had affixed on previous raids before turning them over to the Hot Springs police to destroy.

After setting those machines aside to be used as evidence against local police corruption, Colonel Davis hauled the others out to a gravel pit. There, under the camera eyes of the news media, he ordered a bulldozer driven over the gambling devices until they were metal rubble. Thirty gallons of diesel fuel were then poured over the remains and set to blazing. After the fire died away, the bulldozer buried the blackened bits of metal under a cover of earth. Colonel Davis's final comment was succinct: "This is the end of an era."

Apparently a goodly number of Hot Springs citizens agreed with him. Once again the gluttonous gamblers, as they had done in the days of Flynn-Doran, had tried to swallow too much.

Above: Dismantling of the Southern Club sign, 1971. (Mark Palmer Collection)

As always, however, there were skeptics. "I've been here all my life," state senator Q. Byrum Hurst told a reporter from the *Arkansas Gazette*, "and I've seen this all happen before. I've seen gambling machines hauled out and burned at the fairgrounds and I've seen them come back.

"This may be new to Mr. Rockefeller. This may be new to Mr. Davis, but not to us who have lived here always. Davis will find he can't take carnality out of human beings."

The most widely accepted of *gamen* activities by the general public is horse racing. Individuals who because of moral principles would not set foot in a gambling casino will happily attend a race track and place modest wagers without a twinge of conscience. Perhaps the outdoor atmosphere, the natural surroundings of grass and trees and open sky, combined with the beauty of sleek thoroughbreds in motion, all serve to create an atmosphere of wholesomeness that nullifies any lingering Puritanical guilt over betting. At any rate, throughout the past century (with a few enforced lapses) horse racing has been one of the leading amenities offered visitors to America's Spa.

Even before the calamitous Civil War of 1861-65, which almost destroyed the embryonic settlement of Hot Springs, farm boys from the nearby countryside occasionally brought their fastest-footed ponies into town to race them for the mutual pleasure of residents and visiting health seekers. According to legend, the gathering place for these informal contests was on level pastureland about where Oaklawn Park is now located.

Formalized jockey club racing was introduced during those glamorous years of the Gay Nineties when the nation's cosmopolites swarmed to the Springs. In 1893, Sportsman Park, a half-mile track with four hundred boxed stalls, was built on the southeastern edge of town. An extension of the street railway enabled spectators to reach the race track from downtown Central Avenue in about half an hour. The success of the first season encouraged turfmen from the North to plan for longer meetings with larger purses. In 1895, a name that has been synonymous with Hot Springs racing through three generations was listed among the planners. He was Louis Cella.

Unfortunately for promoters and followers of the sport, state gambling laws began acting as a damper on efforts to improve the quality of the entries and the facilities of the track. In 1903, the state legislature was finally persuaded to repeal the obstructionist laws and the Western Jockey Club, whose board of stewards included Louis Cella, authorized the Hot Springs Jockey Club to prepare for a long meet early in 1904.

The local club's directors worked feverishly through December to insure completion of a grandstand and race track near Lawrence Station on the Choctaw Railroad (successor to the Diamond Jo and predecessor of the Rock Island). During the first racing meet, the railroad agreed to run twelve trains a day from its Hot Springs station. For a while the race track was known as Camp Lawrence, but eventually was given the more dignified name of Essex Park.

Opening day was set for February 25, the season to run through March 19. Mayor George Belding declared February 25 a half-holiday, and a crowd of three thousand came by train to overflow the 200-foot-long grandstand. The 23-day meet was so successful that a group of St. Louis turfmen decided to build a rival track at Oaklawn which was much closer to the center of the city. Its glass-enclosed and steam-heated grandstand had 1,500 seats.

In 1905 Hot Springs enjoyed an overabundance of race meets—the first at Essex Park, the second at Oaklawn, and then a

Above: Bird's-eye view of Essex Park, Hot Springs Jockey Club. (Mary D. Hudgins Collection)

short third sponsored by the Arkansas Jockey Club of Little Rock which brought the Arkansas Derby to Hot Springs for the first time. There were so many horses in town that Simon Cooper, an enterprising owner of a livery stable on Malvern Avenue, opened a bath house for race horses, piping thermal waters from Hot Springs Mountain into a large pool for the exclusive pleasure of thoroughbreds.

Intense rivalry between Essex Park and Oaklawn now began to develop. The Western Jockey Club which assigned racing dates to Arkansas also controlled Oaklawn, and naturally that track was given the best weather dates. In 1906, the rebellious owners of Essex Park joined a group known as the American Turf Association. The result was an overlapping schedule, both tracks being assigned the same days in March for their 1907 season. At a disadvantage because of their more distant location, the Essex Park managers attempted a compromise with their Oaklawn rivals, but were unsuccessful. Consequently Essex Park withdrew for the season, and its owners soon afterward initiated bankruptcy proceedings.

Whatever euphoria the Oaklawn owners may have felt over their victory soon vanished. The year 1907 turned out to be a disaster for Arkansas horse racing enthusiasts. During the previous winter a reform organization had begun a campaign "to drive every racing interest from the state," and was successfully lobbying the state legislature. Surprisingly, one of the leaders of this anti-racing movement was a former turfman himself, the first owner of Essex Park, William McGuigan. He was known as "Umbrella Bill" because he always carried an umbrella, rain or shine, and used it as a luck piece, thrusting it like a rapier from the railing toward whatever horse he was betting on.

Why McGuigan was trying to outlaw his favorite form of recreation is not clear. Possibly he was jealous over the success of his Oaklawn rivals. He claimed he was acting only in the interests of clean racing. Although he had sold Essex Park a couple of years earlier, he had included a clause in the deal that would bring the property back to him if the new owners failed to hold race meets for at least five years. Possibly McGuigan may have been engaging in a bit of clever Machiavellian maneuvering, in a craftiness that has often been typical of those controlling the Spa's more profitable commercial amenities.

At any rate the anti-racing forces won their campaign in the legislature, and betting on horses was banned at Hot Springs for a much longer period than "Umbrella Bill" probably foresaw. The new law was scarcely hours old when police invaded the betting enclosure at Oaklawn and arrested several track employes and officials, including Louis Cella. Although Cella and his associates continued holding races for the remaining three weeks of the 1907 season, all public betting ended. This effectively closed down both Oaklawn and Essex the following year.

For almost a decade the American Spa endured without musical calls to the post, the chatter of tipsters, the pounding of hooves, and the roar of the crowd. Oaklawn did not go entirely unused during this period, however. For a few days each year the Arkansas State Fair was held there. And then in 1916, the city's Business Men's League voted 387 to 13 to revive horse racing with a thirty-day meet at Oaklawn. To avoid legal problems the sponsors announced that the meet would be entirely non-profit. Although there was no pari-mutuel betting, an oral system was permitted.

In spite of these impediments, the season was considered a success, and in 1917 the dates were divided between Oaklawn and

Right: Paddock, Essex Park. (Cook Collection, courtesy of Keeneland Library of Lexington, Ky.)

Below: Race start, Essex Park. (Cook Collection, courtesy of Keeneland Library of Lexington, Ky.)

a completely refurbished Essex Park. The ill luck which had haunted Essex Park from its beginnings was repeated; fire completely destroyed the grandstand the day after its gala re-opening. That was the end of Essex Park as a race track, and a few years later the rising waters of Lake Catherine claimed part of its grounds.

Oaklawn survived, of course, but the anti-racing forces closed it down during the nation's Prohibition Era, that strange period from 1919 to the early 1930's with its contradictory lists of forbidden pleasures that permitted jazz, flappers, bathtub gin and slot machines, but no pari-mutuel racing at the American Spa.

At last in 1934 came the end of Prohibition and arrival of the New Deal with its lifting of national spirits as the great economic depression eased. In keeping with these changes, the Arkansas legislature made pari-mutuel betting legal again at Hot Springs. Year by year after that, attendance increased at Oaklawn, and not a decade passed without major improvements both practical and aesthetic. In 1961, the standard thirty-day meets increased to forty-three. And in 1968, Charles Cella became president, the only fourth-generation racing executive in America. Presently, for fifty-six days every year, as winter withdraws and spring brings blossoms to the green landscaped ellipse within the tawny track, the sport of kings with all its distinctive colors and sounds and aromas becomes the ruling amenity at the American Spa.

Below: Oaklawn, 1905. (Garland Co. Historical Society)

Below: 1874 photo of Valley Street showing Hale House. (Garland Co. Historical Society)

Below: Earl House, c. 1860. (Arkansas History Commission)

The key to any city's level of glamor is the quality of its hotels. As has been noted, Joseph and Nancy Mellard opened the first one in 1820, followed by Ludovicus Belding's more elegant establishment of the 1830's. In 1835 James Conway, who was Arkansas's first governor, joined Samuel Reyburn in building an inn adjacent to their bath house, and advertised its "well furnished Bar" and "abundance of Horse-feed." Henry M. Rector, a future governor and a cousin of Conway, opened the Tavern House in 1850. During that decade the hotels of Hot Springs won some admiration for their cuisine. "Their tables are well supplied with venison, bear meat, fish and fowl, in addition to supplies from New Orleans and other places," one visitor commented. "The charges are $25 a month."

In 1852, Stidham's Hotel announced the addition of "a well-filled ice house, a luxury heretofore unknown at this place." Three years later the management bragged of having forty or fifty tons of ice, making it possible to add "an Ice Cream Saloon Soda Fountain" to the hostelry's amenities.

During the post-war renaissance there was a shortage of quality hotels until the 1870's when the luxury-loving Sam Fordyce offered to help finance construction of the Arlington. At that time the Rector House at the north end of Bath House Row was the only hotel on reservation land. With William Gaines and Samuel Stitt as partners, Fordyce built the largest hotel in

Right: Advertisement for Hot Springs Hotel at Malvern from *Hot Springs Illustrated Monthly*, 1879. (Walter Nunn Collection)

Hot Springs Hotel.
MALVERN, ARKANSAS.
JOS. SIGEMUNT - - - Proprietor;
HERMAN HARTSON, Clerk.

First-class house in every respect. Sample rooms and special rates for commercial travelers. Meals for Fifty Cents. Passengers from Hot Springs going North, will arrive at Malvern at 12:40, and will have 40 minutes for dinner—which they can get at this hotel, near the depot, for 50c; thus saving 25c per meal, and getting quite as good fare as at Little Rock, or elsewhere on the road.

Arkansas around the old Rector and named it the Arlington. Guest rooms were lighted with gas, and occupants could signal the main desk with an electrical-powered bell. A first-rate dining hall and a large ballroom for social functions were also features of the new hotel.

During the 1880's the Arlington's chief rival was the Avenue on Park Avenue. It boasted of a hydraulic elevator and electric lights in the dining room. The Hay House, a four-story brick at Division and Park, installed water-closets on every floor, and was "the only hotel in Hot Springs heated by steam." The Waverly, on the east side of Park, had hair mattresses on its beds. Its elevator was equipped with an air-cushion, "making it absolutely safe," and for guests traveling to and from bath houses, the management furnished a closed carriage to prevent "liability of taking cold after bathing."

The United States Hotel, built in 1888 across Central Avenue from Bath House Row, joined the Hay House in the change from wooden structures to brick. In that same year, *Cutter's Guide to Hot Springs* listed fourteen additional hotels, the minimum rates ranging from $17.50 per week at the fashionable Arlington to $5.00 per week at the Exchange. Another hotel popular with travelers journeying to and from the Spa was the Hot Springs Hotel located near the Iron Mountain Railroad depot in Malvern. Here they could spend the night if they missed connections, or enjoy a meal for fifty cents while waiting for a late train.

Above: Samuel H. Stitt. (Garland Co. Historical Society)

Below: The Arlington Hotel from *Cutter's Guide to the Hot Springs of Arkansas*, 1887. (Mary D. Hudgins Collection)

Right: The Avenue Hotel from *Cutter's Guide to the Hot Springs of Arkansas*, 1887. (Mary D. Hudgins Collection)

Above: Hotel Hay from *Cutter's Guide to the Hot Springs of Arkansas*, 1887. (Mary D. Hudgins Collection)

Right: The New Waverly Hotel from *Nature's Wonderland, Cutter's Guide to the Hot Springs of Arkansas*, 1884. (Mary D. Hudgins Collection)

Right: United States Hotel from *Cutter's Guide to the Hot Springs of Arkansas*, 1887. (Mary D. Hudgins Collection)

RATE OF CHARGING FOR BOARDING PER WEEK.		
The Arlington	$17 50 to	$21 00
Avenue Hotel	15 00 "	20 00
Sumpter House	12 50 "	21 00
Waverly House	12 50 "	25 00
Hay House	12 00 "	18 00
French's Hotel	10 00 "	15 00
Barnes' House	10 00 "	18 00
Clifton House	8 00 "	16 00
Claybrook House	9 00 "	12 00
Akin House	7 00 "	10 00
Windsor	10 00 "	17 50
Clarendon	10 00 "	18 00
Sage's Hotel	3 00 "	10 00
St. James	7 00 "	10 00
Glendale House	8 00 "	9 00
Gaines' Cottage	8 00 "	10 00
Branch House	8 00 "	10 00
Commercial Hotel	7 00 "	15 00
Exchange Hotel	5 00 "	6 00
Rice's Hotel	5 00 "	8 00

Above: Hotel rates from *Nature's Wonderland, Cutter's Guide to the Hot Springs of Arkansas*, 1884. (Mary D. Hudgins Collection)

Right: Arlington Hotel fire, photos by Too Cute Studio, April 5, 1923. (Garland Co. Historical Society)

To meet increasing competition, the Arlington's management was constantly refitting and enlarging its facilities and introducing new thermal bath equipment so that its guests could "take the cure" without ever leaving the hotel's boundaries. In 1893 the owners decided the time had come to raze the old patchwork structure and build a completely new hotel on its exclusive and highly prized site on government reservation land. The result was a twin-towered four-story building of red brick, described as "of the Moorish design," or "Spanish renaissance." Guests were impressed by its magnificent chandeliers, massive fireplaces, oak-finished walls, sun-porches and verandas.

By the early 1920's the new Arlington's three hundred rooms were insufficient to accommodate the numbers of visitors who wanted to stay there. The owners were in the midst of plans for an annex to be built across Fountain Street when an unexpected conflagration on April 5, 1923, changed everything. In early afternoon the Arlington's head waiter, W. M. Acree, discovered a smoldering electrical fire in a basement grill. Smoke drifted upstairs, but the guests were slow to depart because they believed they could exit at any time from every level to Hot Springs Mountain. As it turned out, about fifty were trapped and had to leave by fire department ladders. William Pinkerton, head of the famed detective agency, who was there for the baths, was so cocksure of his and the hotel's invulnerability that he sat on the front veranda complacently smoking a cigar and watching efforts of the firemen until it was too late to rescue his possessions from his room.

That evening while the remains of the Arlington sank into ashes, Pinkerton along with many other guests had to take up quarters in the Eastman, the largest hotel in the city, which was owned by some of the directors of the Arlington—familiar names such as Stitt, Fordyce and Gaines. Located across Reserve Avenue from the Army and Navy Hospital, the Eastman catered to families. It was called "the Monarch of the Glen," and was widely known for its musical concerts and social gatherings. During World War II the Eastman was acquired by the War Department, connected to the hospital by an overhead passage, and used to house the overflow of hospital patients. The Hot Springs Post Office and Federal Building now stand on its site.

Above: Arlington Hotel fire, 1923. (Garland Co. Historical Society)

Right: (from left to right) Will J. Davis, Dr. Chamberlain, Billy Pinkerton, Billy Maurice. (Mary D. Hudgins Collection)

Meanwhile after serving the public for half a century on government reservation land, the owners of the Arlington decided to give up the hotel's unique but inadequate site. The ground was converted into the present-day Arlington Park. The third and largest Arlington Hotel was then built across Fountain Street where it now dominates Central Avenue with its eleven-story central section. The hotel is one of the more popular choices for conventions in America, with its grand lobby and spacious rooms for dining and meetings.

During the first half of the 20th century the Arlington's chief rivals were the Eastman, the Majestic and the Park. The Park on Malvern Avenue was surrounded by four acres of trees, shrubs, flowers and fountains. To attract "ladies and children unaccompanied by husband or father," playgrounds, lawns for croquet, and tennis courts were provided. Other attractions also included a glassed sun pavilion atop the Park's six floors affording guests a spectacular view of the surrounding mountains.

Successor to the fabulous Avenue Hotel of the 80's and 90's was the Majestic, which first came into being in 1902 as a four-story brick building at Whittington and Park. In 1926 the Majestic's owners acquired the Hiram Whittington home site and built an eight-story addition. Since that time several other expansions have occurred.

Below: Cover for Hot Springs pamphlet featuring the three great hotels. (Garland Co. Historical Society)

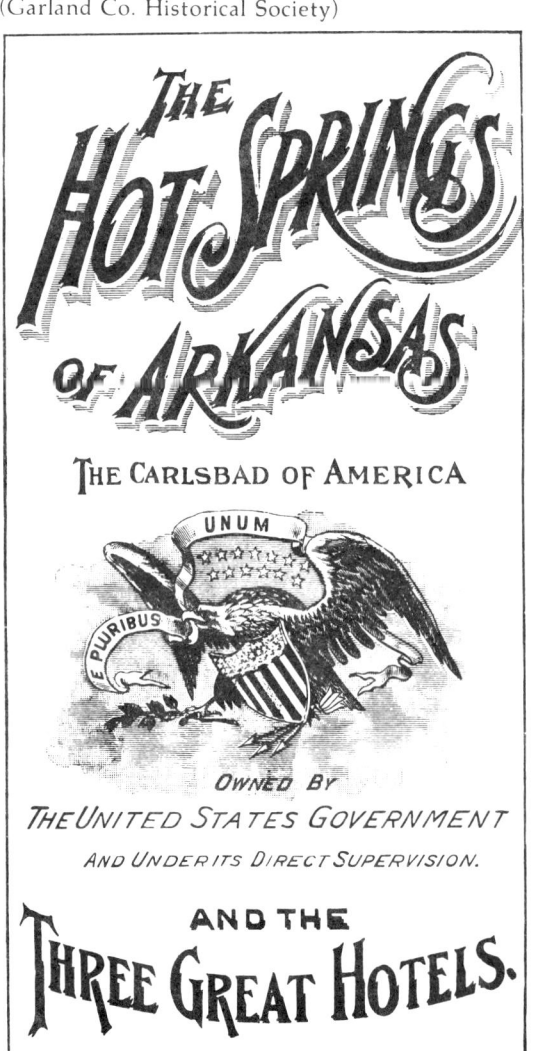

Above: The Eastman Tower and view looking south from the tower. Both images from *Hot Springs, Arkansas, The Carlsbad of America*, 1893. (Hot Springs National Park)

Above: Park Hotel from *Hot Springs Illustrated Journal*, August 1891. (Garland Co. Historical Society)

Left: Arlington Hotel dining room, 1938. (Hot Springs Chamber of Commerce)

Below: Arlington Hotel. (Hot Springs Chamber of Commerce)

Left: Hotel Eastman from *Hot Springs Illustrated Journal*, August 1891. (Garland Co. Historical Society)

Because the 19th century was male-oriented, so were most of the amenities of the time. But this attitude began to change at the American Spa as the city moved prosperously into the 20th century. The quality hotels paved the way, gearing their services toward families, and then all through the valley commercial amusements began springing up, their appeal aimed toward young families rather than to adult males. Before the turn of the century Norman McLeod opened an amusement park up on Fountain Street that was supposed to bear his name. For its sixty or so years of existence, however, to every visitor young and old the place was Happy Hollow. David Anselberg bought out McLeod before the first World War, and his additions to the park made Happy Hollow the Spa's main attraction for family groups, especially during the 1920's. It had burros, a small zoo, corny signs, garish souvenirs, and a remarkably surrealistic photograph gallery where one could assume a dozen different identities by posing with only the head showing through a rounded aperture of some incongruous painted scene. Or a youngster could pose upon the back of a real live burro and then send postcard prints home to show off to envious friends and relatives.

Above: Sun parlor, Lamar Bath House, 1905. (Mary D. Hudgins Collection)

Below: Shooting Gallery at Happy Hollow. (Garland Co. Historical Society)

Below: Scenes in Happy Hollow from *Hot Springs, Arkansas, The Carlsbad of America*, 1893. (Hot Springs National Park)

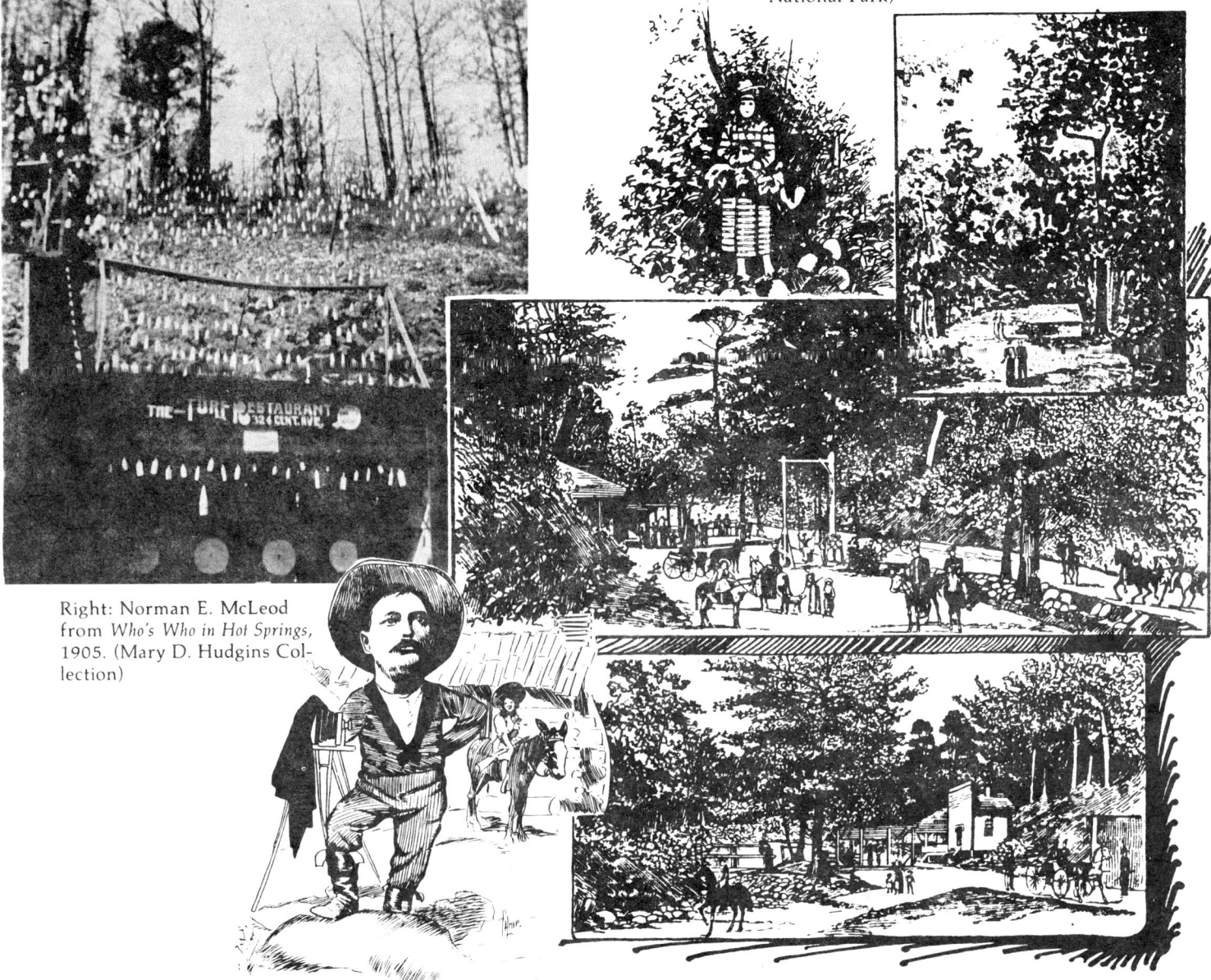

Right: Norman E. McLeod from *Who's Who in Hot Springs*, 1905. (Mary D. Hudgins Collection)

Above: Bird's-eye view of Hot Springs from the mountain observatory from *Frank Leslie's Illustrated Newspaper*, March 31, 1888. (Mary D. Hudgins Collection)

A burro could also be hired for a slow ride up Hot Springs Mountain to the observation tower, a highlight of any visit to the Spa. In the 1870's Ellis Woolman, who also published the *Weekly Sentinel*, built at the summit a wooden tower eighty feet high, equipped with a large telescope. After climbing a stairway, observers could see for thirty miles, which was an exciting experience before the invention of the airplane. In 1906 the decaying wooden structure was replaced by a 165-foot steel tower equipped with an elevator. After many years of service it too was declared unsafe and removed in 1971. In 1982 work was begun on a third tower, this one to be 180 feet high.

Below: Second Hot Springs tower, 1952. (Mary D. Hudgins Collection)

Above: Burro rides at Happy Hollow. (Mary D. Hudgins Collection)

Above: Mrs. Thomas Cockburn and son Edwin pose in ostrich cart. (Garland Co. Historical Society)

Early in this century, first-time visitors to Hot Springs were sometimes startled by the sight of an enormous ostrich harnessed to a cart dashing spiritedly along Central Avenue. This was a surefire advertising stunt devised by Thomas Cockburn who in 1900 brought three hundred ostriches to the Spa and opened a 27-acre Ostrich Farm out on Whittington Avenue. Cockburn trained his big birds to race, carry children on their backs, and entertain a daily succession of spectators.

Probably inspired by Cockburn's success, H. L. Campbell in 1902 imported fifty alligators, a number which soon grew to several hundred, and opened an Alligator Farm nearby the Ostrich Farm. Campbell built a high chute for his reptiles to perform upon, and also sold such byproducts as alligator suitcases, alligator purses, and alligator teeth. For a dollar one could purchase a baby alligator to take home and raise as a pet.

With these commercial enterprises, and an amusement park for picnicking, riding a merry-go-round, playing various games, or listening to band concerts, Whittington Avenue offered an abundance of amenities for the young at heart. There was something magical in a streetcar named "Whittington," and although few riders knew the origin of the name, on fine days young children and their parents filled the trolleys to capacity. Like old Hiram Whittington they were pioneers of a sort, setting the pattern for the Spa's family-oriented recreation of today.

Although the Alligator Farm still flourishes, Happy Hollow and the Ostrich Farm no longer exist. Through the years, however, other entertainments have come to take their places in a different and faster-paced world—Tussaud's Wax Museum, Animal Wonderland, the I. Q. Zoo, Magic Springs Family Fun Park, and Tiny Town, a miniature animated village. For seasonal attractions, the Spa no longer has the Arkansas State Fair which started at Oaklawn and reached its high point with a visit by President Theodore Roosevelt in 1910 before it was transferred to Little Rock. A more glamorous seasonal affair is the Miss Arkansas Pageant which Hot Springs began hosting in 1958. Five years later, in 1963, the judges chose Donna Axum to be Miss Arkansas, and she went on to become Miss America. In 1981 Elizabeth Ward of Russellville began a similar triumph at the Spa's summer pageant.

Below: Alligator slide, amusement at Alligator Farm. (Garland Co. Historical Society)

Above: Grandstand at Whittington Park filled to view bicycle races, 1897. (Garland Co. Historical Society)

Below: Alligator Farm postcard. (Hot Springs National Park)

The most unique of all diversions for all members of a family is the Mid-America Center, a perfect combination of beguiling and instructive exhibits, most of which require some participation from those who visit the challenging museum. Conceived with the aid of specialists from the Smithsonian Institution in Washington and constructed by the State of Arkansas, the Center is now sponsored by the city of Hot Springs.

From the beginning the Spa has stimulated visitors with intellectual and artistic challenges. In the early years scientists came to study the springs and rock formations, and in later years health seekers were delighted to find artists and craftsmen producing a wide range of creative objects. Clay formations in the area provided materials for excellent pottery; painters found the scenery and the climate conducive to both outdoor and studio work; handicraft artisans had easy access to a variety of native materials.

Below: The Mid-America Center Museum, 1982. (Pittman and Associates)

Above: Ouachita Pottery, 1877. (Mary D. Hudgins Collection)

CHARLES CUTTER,
Real Estate Broker,
AND
General Agent.

Buys, Sells Rents and Exchanges Houses and Lots in

HOT SPRINGS,

And Farming and Wild Lands in

Arkansas and Texas.

Above: Charles Cutter real estate ad, *Hot Springs Illustrated Monthly*, 1879. (Walter Nunn Collection)

Above: Masthead for Charles Cutter's *Hot Springs Illustrated Monthly*. (Walter Nunn Collection)

Below: Charles Cutter. (Mary D. Hudgins Collection)

Above: Guide books to Hot Springs published by Charles Cutter. (Mary D. Hudgins Collection)

In 1869 when the reviving town's population was but little more than a thousand and the surrounding townships not more more than twice that, W. G. Musgrove and J. D. Hutson boldly started a newspaper, the *Courier*, to inform citizens and visitors of events near and far. Musgrove and Hutson had the field to themselves until 1873 when the *Times* began publishing. In those days newspapers were the chief means of communication, although many were short-lived. The *Courier* and *Times* died, and the *Sentinel* and *News* were born. In 1899 John Higgins started the *Record*, later merging it with the *Sentinel*, the combination continuing to this day. Several other papers came and went, notably the *Horseshoe* and the *Hornet*, which originally were on opposite sides of the early gambling wars. They later merged, became the *Daily News*, finally winding up in John Riggs' *New Era*.

Magazines have also had their day in Hot Springs. One of the most impressive in appearance was Charles Cutter's *Hot Springs Illustrated Monthly*, a folio-sized periodical filled with lively text and exquisite line drawings made from photographs, mostly scenes and buildings in and around the Spa. Occasionally pictures from other Arkansas cities were included. "Our size is now the same as 'Harper's Weekly,'" Cutter wrote on the occasion of the magazine's first anniversary, "and we hope our efforts to be worthy the patronage of the citizens of Arkansas, and especially those of Hot Springs, will not be in vain."

Charles Cutter was an ailing native of New York City who heard about the healing waters of Hot Springs in 1873, and made the long journey by rail. His cure was rapid and complete, and although he was well along into his thirties, he moved his family down from New York and began earning a living by publishing his now famed *Guide to Hot Springs*, revising regularly to keep them up to date, from 1874 to 1912, the year he died. For a short time after that his son John carried on the tradition. If any man deserves to have a statue on Central Avenue, Charles Cutter is a prime candidate for the honor. His guides and the short-lived *Illustrated Monthly* spread the legend of the Spa across America. Bath houses and hotels presented the guides to guests, and many a visitor purchased extra copies to send or take home to friends. With the guide's fiftieth edition in 1908, Cutter's total press run passed 758,000 copies. Today, as a repository of Hot Springs history both in words and pictures a file of Cutter's *Guides* is without parallel.

Another magazine that was indigenous to Hot Springs and probably would have thrived nowhere else was the *Arkansaw Thomas Cat*. It was the creation of Jefferson Davis Orear, a Kentuckian who ran away to Venezuela at an early age, but eventually returned to work for several Missouri newspapers. On Thanksgiving Day 1889 he visited Hot Springs and was so charmed by Bath House Row that he resolved to make the Spa his home. He started publishing his weekly magazine in 1890, and it appeared fairly regularly until the economic depression of the 1930's.

The cover was dominated by a huge cat, almost in an attack position, and in the background were small drawings of the legendary Arkansas Traveler on horseback and the cabin of the fiddler. Orear emblazoned the rest of the cover with mottoes: A JOURNALISTIC HIGHBALL RUN BY A HEATHEN. GOD HELP THE RICH, THE POOR CAN BEG. ITS PRINCIPLE—ELEVATION OF HORSE THIEVES AND PUBLIC MORALS. IT BELIEVES IN ONE COUNTRY, ONE FLAG, AND ONE WIFE AT A TIME. LOVE YOUR FRIENDS AND BRIMSTONE YOUR ENEMIES. *The Arkansaw Thomas Cat's* humor, generated almost entirely by its iconclast editor, was of its time, and its vogue declined in the way that all facets of popular culture fade before changing attitudes of the public.

Above: Jefferson Davis Orear from *History of the Arkansas Press for 100 Years and More*, Fred W. Allsopp, 1922. (Walter Hussman)

Left: *Arkansaw Thomas Cat*. (Mary D. Hudgins Collection)

Concurrent with its recreation facilities, the Spa has always provided visitors with most of the conveniences and comforts of our technological age almost as soon as they are made available anywhere else. "We found the city lighted by gas," a surprised Yankee reported in 1875, and only seven years later the Hot Springs Electric Company was formed to provide that mysterious new source of illumination and energy. In 1880, only four years after Alexander Graham Bell demonstrated his telephone at the Centennial Exposition in Philadelphia, a line was run from W. L. Little's grocery store on Central Avenue to Little Rock, connecting the Spa's voices with those of the outside world.

Strangely enough, however, the institution of banking was slow to reach the city. The leading merchants operated their own cumbersome monetary exchange systems, but for residents and visitors the lack of banks must have indeed been a severe inconvenience. The era of barter described by Hiram Whittington in the 1830's was no longer practicable after the Civil War. And as we have seen, travelers to the Spa who were aware of the town's lack of banks inevitably tempted stagecoach robbers and other miscreants by carrying large sums of money on their persons. Not until 1874 was the first small bank organized by two men from St. Louis. Soon others followed, including the Arkansas National in 1882, and the Arkansas Trust Company in 1907. Under the direction of Cecil Cupp, the latter became the Arkansas Bank and Trust Company in 1961 and Arkansas' largest state-chartered bank in 1972.

Being a town where the ailing come to recover, the healing arts were always foremost among its accommodations. In addition to the Army and Navy Hospital, three additional sanitariums and infirmaries were built before 1900. In 1914 the B'nai Brith opened its Leo N. Levi Memorial Hospital, with emphasis upon research in the treatment of arthritis, and during the 1950's after the demise of the Free Bath House, the Libbey Memorial was developed into a modern physical therapy center.

Below: Arkansas National Bank from *Cutter's Guide to the Hot Springs of Arkansas*, 1887. (Mary D. Hudgins Collection)

Below: Cecil Cupp, Sr. (Arkansas Bank and Trust)

Above: Dave Burgauer. (James B. Dowds)

Nor was the spiritual side of life neglected in fun-loving Hot Springs. In 1838, thanks to the efforts of Sarah Hale, wife of the rambunctious John C., the Baptists built the first church. It was made of logs, with split-log seats, and stood in the general area of the present-day First National Bank. Burned by guerrillas during Civil War times, the church was rebuilt near the south end of Bath House Row, and then again at Prospect and Quapaw. Although the Methodists were the first to send itinerant preachers to Hot Springs, they did not build a church until 1855 (also in the Bath House Row area) and then in 1871 moved to Central Avenue and Chapel. Other denominations soon followed, the Catholics in 1870, the Presbyterians in 1876, and so on until at present about eighty churches are represented at the American Spa.

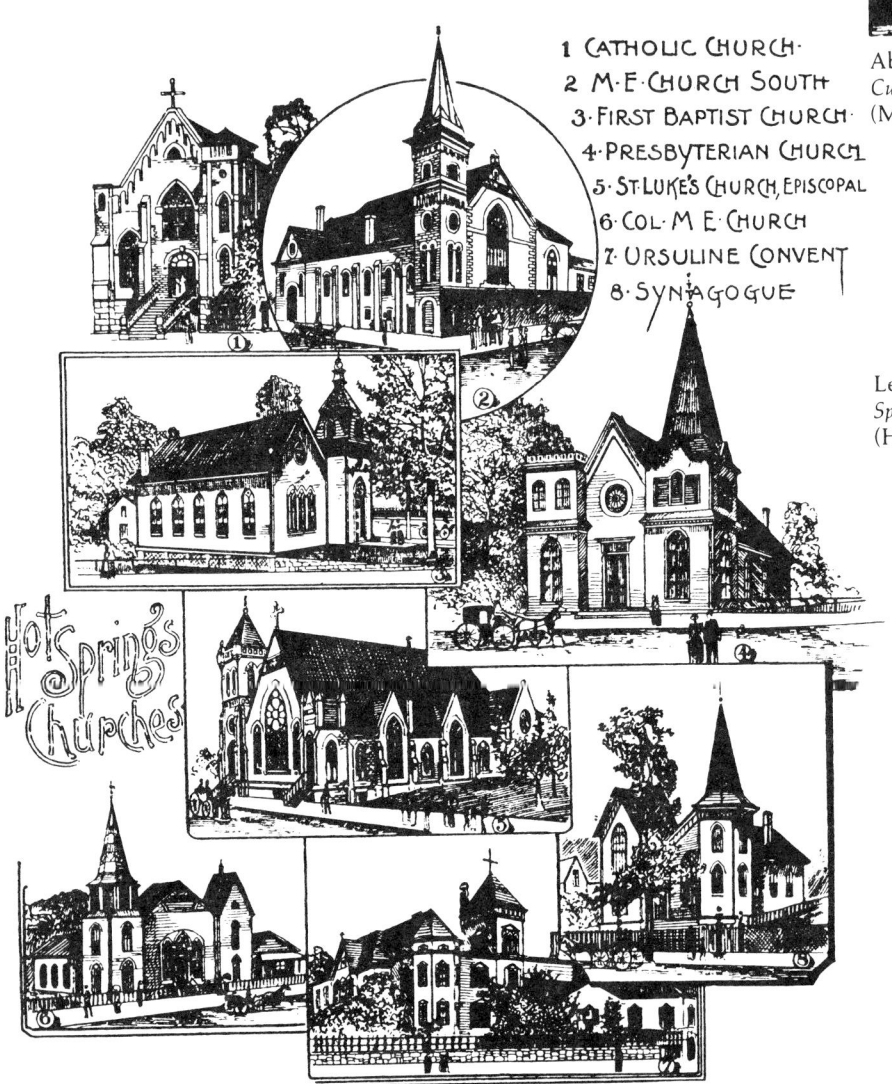

Above: Baptist Church and Masonic Hall from *Cutter's Guide to the Hot Springs of Arkansas*, 1877. (Mary D. Hudgins Collection)

Left: Group of Hot Springs churches from *Hot Springs, Arkansas, The Carlsbad of America*, 1893. (Hot Springs National Park)

CHAPTER V

INHABITANTS

"I was born in Hot Springs and lived here all my life. I wouldn't live anywhere else."

Below: Charles N. Rockafellow came to Hot Springs in 1868, established a drug store. Later he was proprietor of the Rockafellow Bath House and the Rockafellow Hotel and Apartments, from the *Centennial History of Arkansas* by Dallas Herndon. (Charles Witsell, Jr.)

Living in Hot Springs has always had a special quality about it. Midway down through the sesquicentennial years of the Spa, there was a popular saying that no native lived in Hot Springs; everyone came from somewhere else. This is no longer true, of course. A certain retired gentleman of today who can be seen walking the Grand Promenade almost every morning and evening will reply to anyone who asks him: "I was born in Hot Springs and lived here all my life. I wouldn't live anywhere else. I've been to California and a few other places, but they don't interest me much."

The first waves of settlers came from much wider geographical sources and from much greater distances than the settlers of other towns in the region. Until America moved well into the 20th century, local customs and attitudes around the nation were far more varied than they are now. Consequently the permanent inhabitants of the Spa had to learn to accept from their neighbors vastly different habits, religions, morals, dress, likes, dislikes, and speech patterns. This may account for the city's long-standing record of tolerance for things that are different, and an

Right: Circa 1877 photo of Valley Street with Rockafellow's drugstore and an early circulating library. (Garland Co. Historical Society)

ability to adjust readily to forces that might have overwhelmed other communities. People with roots in various foreign countries and states as diverse as Illinois, Missouri, Texas, Tennessee, Ohio, New York, Nebraska, Massachusetts, Iowa and Georgia would have found life unendurable together without forbearance, constant compromises, and occasional reconciliations.

From the years of pioneer Hiram Whittington of Massachusetts, the Spa always had citizens who moved it along, some out of hopes for personal gain, others because of a thirst for power, others because they truly loved the town and wanted it to prosper, yet whether it prospered or not would have chosen to live nowhere else. To try to name all the outstanding citizens would be impossible. Several have been mentioned earlier, and space permits only a brief sampling of others.

The superintendents of the reservation—and the later national park—often demonstrated as much or more civic pride than the town's elected mayors. In early times the superintendents also had access to considerably more funds than did the city officials. General Benjamin F. Kelley, a West Virginian, was the first superintendent. He had the onerous task of clearing squatters from the reservation, but was compassionate enough to set aside a special area between Reserve and Springs streets for temporary tents and shacks. As a dubious reward for magnanimity the townspeople named the place "Kelleytown."

Colonel Samuel Hamblen succeeded Kelley in 1882. Hamblen was a topographical engineer from Maine, and had previously served on the reservation survey commission. Outspoken with his opinions, Hamblen described one of his fellow commissioners as petty and worthless, another as ignorant, a third as grasping for some of the government land. Hamblen fought for and obtained federal funds to pay for covering Hot Springs Creek and creating present-day Central Avenue.

General Charles Fields from Georgia, a West Point graduate and Confederate Army veteran, took over in 1885. Fields resisted all interference from the government of Arkansas in his operation of the reservation, but he was usually overruled by the Interior Department. In 1889 Colonel Frank Thompson, also a Confederate veteran, was the first Arkansan appointed to the office. He initiated a number of construction projects in the park and built the first official superintendent's residence on Fountain Street. In 1893 Colonel William J. Little, a Hot Springs resident, began an active seven-year term during which he led an arduous campaign against the "doctor drummers." He strengthened the reservation's ties with the city, and introduced attractive features such as hot water fountains along the sidewalks.

Martin A. Eisele, an Ohioan who arrived in Hot Springs in 1877 to become a pharmacist, broke the string of superintendents with military titles when President McKinley appointed him to office in 1900. Eisele completed Little's efforts to end the "drumming" nuisance, and arranged for the first official analysis of the thermal waters by the U.S. Bureau of Chemistry. He also succeeded in obtaining long overdue funds for modernizing roads and trails on Hot Springs Mountain.

With the growth of the city, the relative power of the park superintendents began to decline, but most of them have always been viewed as innovative community leaders. Donald S. Libbey, a Missourian, served longer than any other superintendent—from the 1930's through the 1950's, with occasional brief assignments elsewhere. He was one of the most admired for his enthusiasm, his attachment to the Spa, and his support of physical therapy. After his death in 1959, the Libbey Memorial Physical Medicine Center was named for him.

Above: Martin A. Eisele. (Garland Co. Historical Society)

Below: Professional "advertisements" from *Hot Springs Illustrated Monthly*, 1879. (Walter Nunn Collection)

Professional Cards.

T. B. BUCHANAN, M. D.,

HOT SPRINGS ....ARK.

DR. JNO. B BROOKS,

Consulting Physician,

[Homœopathist]

HOT SPRINGS .... ARK.

H. M. RECTOR, JR., M. D.,

Resident Physician,

HOT SPRINGS......ARKANSAS.

W. H. BARRY, M. D.,

HOT SPRINGS, ARK.

SIDNEY W. FRANKLIN, M. D.,

Resident Physician,

HOT SPRINGS .... ARK.

GEO. W. LAWRENCE, M. D.,

Resident Physician,

HOT SPRINGS .... ARK.

P. H. ELLSWORTH, M. D.,

Resident Physician,

HOT SPRINGS, ARK.

L. S. ORDWAY, M. D.,

RESIDENT

HOMŒOPATHIC PHYSICIAN,

HOT SPRINGS...............ARK.

Above: Hot Springs Reservation Administration Building. (Mary D. Hudgins Collection)

Below: J. J. Sutton's Novaculite Quarry No. 7 from *Geological Survey of Arkansas*, 1890. (Garland Co. Historical Society)

The presence of the reservation has always provided employment for a number of Hot Springs inhabitants, directly and indirectly. Even before it became a national park on March 4, 1921, the superintendents employed lawmen known as Reservation Police, outfitting them with brass-buttoned blue-serge uniforms. They wore brass badges on their coats and official insignia across the fronts of their derby hats. The dismounted men patrolled streets bordering the reservation while members of a special unit known as the Mounted Reservation Police used horses to guard the trails and roads and stayed in readiness for emergencies.

In the first censuses of the town and township, most of the inhabitants listed their occupation as farmers or laborers, but as the town grew into the American Spa, service occupations and professions increased at a rapid rate. During the height of Bath House Row's popularity, Hot Springs must have had a higher percentage of medical men in its population than any other city in the nation. The first physician set up practice in 1850 about where Canyon Street now joins Central Avenue. He was Dr. William J. Hammond, a South Carolinian. By the 1880's, Cutter's *Guide* was devoting two or three pages of each edition to listing resident physicians and specialists in various ailments.

Most of the bath houses advised bathers to have a physician prescribe individualized regimes for taking thermal treatments. When this custom became widespread, unqualified and fraudulent doctors found it easy to obtain clients. The Interior Department eventually stepped in and required registration of all resident physicians before authorizing them to prescribe thermal baths.

From the town's beginnings, settlers discovered a ready market for various minerals of the area, notably the quartz crystals known as "Hot Springs diamonds," lodestones from magnetite, and whetstones made from the novaculite that was once so highly prized by the Indians for its hardness. Hiram Whittington, Dr. William Hammond, and Phineas Barnes were among the first to hone novaculite into whetstones and market them as far away as Europe.

Below: Crystal peddler c. 1870-80. (Garland Co. Historical Society)

One of the oldest enterprises in Garland County is Mountain Valley Water, originating from Mountain Valley Springs near Blakely Mountain twelve miles north of Hot Springs. Peter E. Green bought the springs in 1872 and built a large hotel. The water proved to be so popular with visitors who wanted to continue drinking it after returning to their homes that a company was formed in 1883 to bottle and ship it all over the world. Among the founders were names familiar in early Hot Springs history— G. G. Latta, Samuel H. Stitt, and the omnipresent Samuel W. Fordyce. Early in this century it was taken over by the Schlafley family.

Before the inhabitants of Hot Springs stopped constructing their buildings entirely of wood and turned to more permanent materials, they also spent a good deal of their time rebuilding the town. They suffered through three devastating fires in 1878, 1905 and 1913, and many damaging flash floods, the worst in 1923.

The fire of March 5, 1878, started soon after midnight on the east side of Central Avenue when a lamp was overturned in Greenleaf's Bagnio, which was presumably a small bath house although the word has shadier meanings. By the time the town's single piece of horse-drawn fire-fighting equipment arrived on the scene, the blaze had spread to the French Restaurant. Unfortunately the walking-beam hand pump could not draw enough water from muddy Hot Springs Creek to stop the spreading flames. Fire bells brought out most of the able-bodied inhabitants and hotel guests, but bucket brigades also proved ineffectual. Windblown sparks spread the conflagration to the west side of the avenue, and the fire began sweeping northward and southward at the same time.

Frank Stearns, a clerk for the U.S. Hot Springs Commission, had returned to the Arlington Hotel about midnight after attending a dance. He had just fallen asleep when he was awakened and told that he should pack his things and move out. "It looked impossible to save the Arlington," he wrote later. Because many of the other guests were semi-invalids staying at the hotel for the baths, Stearns assisted in the removal of about three

Above: Mountain Valley Bottling Works and motor truck. (Hot Springs National Park)

Below: View of the burned district from *Harper's Weekly*, March 30, 1878. (Mary D. Hudgins Collection)

Above: Early horse-drawn fire equipment. (Garland Co. Historical Society)

Below: 1904 City Hall, Fire Department and Auditorium with "modern" fire trucks. (Garland Co. Historical Society)

Below: Remains of the Methodist Church at the corner of Chapel and Central after the 1905 fire. (Garland Co. Historical Society)

hundred of them. "Then we all awaited the approach of the fire as it moved swiftly up the valley with all ease."

The Arlington was spared, however, as were most of the larger bath houses. A change in the wind's direction helped the bucket brigades bring the fire to a stop before it reached the Big Iron, but it burned on down the valley until almost noon the next day. When it was finally brought under control, the exhausted fire-fighters must have been unable to restore themselves with any sort of drink of alcoholic content. A total of fourteen saloons, possibly all that were licensed in the town, had been reduced to ashes. One of them bore the name of its owner, Jim Lane, who would soon be back in business to set the stage for the Flynn-Doran gambling war of 1884. Other losses included three drug-stores, the offices of nineteen doctors, three livery stables, several restaurants, the *Daily Sentinel* building, the Post Office, the Court House, and the Baptist Church. Four bath houses and seven hotels were destroyed, although only the Hot Springs Hotel on the east side of Central Avenue was a major establishment.

By afternoon of March 6, from the Arlington southward, Hot Springs resembled a city destroyed by total war. All that remained of the ravaged section were a few desolate brick chimneys and building foundations, blackened stumps of trunks of trees, a line of scorched telegraph poles, and bridges collapsed into the ash-filled creek.

"Our beautiful little city is no more," wrote Frank Stearns. He was both right and wrong in his judgment. The old Spa was gone; its departure, however, only made room for the new American Spa which would be rebuilt in time for the Elegant Eighties.

A generation later, on February 26, 1905, the disaster was repeated. In the winter blackness between midnight and dawn, with a cold wind blowing down Central Avenue, a fire started in the 35-year-old Grand Central Hotel on Chapel Street. While fire bells were still sounding the alarm, the flames spread to the Methodist Church at the corner of Central Avenue, then leaped across Chapel to the Plateau Hotel. From that moment on until late morning, the fire twisted like a tornado, consuming both sides of Chapel, turning southward along Quapaw and Prospect, then eastward to Grand Avenue. It crossed Central Avenue, turned north along Broadway, and after completing a circle burned itself out about where it began. Gone were forty square blocks, which included the residences of more than two thousand inhabitants, three hotels, two churches, the court house and jail.

Once again, however, the citizens resolved to rebuild, to recreate the southern part of the Spa. Unfortunately, however, few of the new structures were fire-resistant, and eight years later, on September 5, 1913, south Hot Springs suffered another great conflagration.

Early in the sultry afternoon of that late summer day, a laundress on Church Street left a shirt hanging too close to a charcoal burner, and about two o'clock an alarm brought the first fire engines. This time the flames raced along Malvern Avenue, devouring some of the magnificent homes that had escaped the 1905 fire. The beautiful Park Hotel and its grove of trees were quickly enveloped; the Ozark Sanitarium, the Iron Mountain Railroad depot, the high school, the electric power plant—all vanished as the inferno moved toward Central and Olive. There at the Methodist Church, the fire turned into the rebuilt area along Ouachita and Quapaw, gutting the new court house. By this time a train arrived from Little Rock with relief firemen and equipment. The fire was stopped at Hazel Street, but sparks had set the dry woods on West Mountain to blazing, and not until after midnight was the smoking city free of flames.

Fifty blocks, a thousand buildings, 2,500 homeless—tell the story. One of the most serious losses was the electric plant. For weeks the inhabitants returned to using kerosene lamps and candles for lights, and the old mule-drawn streetcars had to be brought out of storage to replace the electric cars. This time the Spa suffered severe economic dislocations. Many regular visitors, hearing of the disaster, stayed away for one or two seasons, and few new people came. It was during this period that the business men decided to revive horse racing as a means of restoring their lost prosperity. And when rebuilding began, the pace was slower than before; it was as though the builders felt that each new structure must be better, more permanent than the one it replaced.

Upper Central Avenue, which had escaped the great fires of 1905 and 1913, was the victim in 1923 of an unusual occurrence in a town blessed most of the time with gentle weather. After an unusually heavy downpour during the night of May 13, a massive thunderstorm the next day dumped almost six more inches of rain in a short time over the surrounding mountains. Streams poured down every slope, collected in the branches, and brawled headlong for Hot Springs Creek. The archway under Central Avenue swelled to full and could take no more. Then the torrent ripped away pavement, and the avenue became a raging river, sweeping automobiles away, bursting through store fronts, destroying everything in its path. As bad as the flood was, it was not as devastating as the fires. The townspeople went to work, and in a matter of days Central Avenue was back in business, ready for the "roaring Twenties."

Above: Central Ave. looking south during September 5, 1913 fire. Store owners in foreground removing their merchandise ahead of fire. (Garland Co. Historical Society)

Below: Wagons pressed into street railway service after the power plant burned in 1913. (Mary D. Hudgins Collection)

Left: *Sentinel-Record* headline for 1923 fire and flood. (Garland Co. Historical Society)

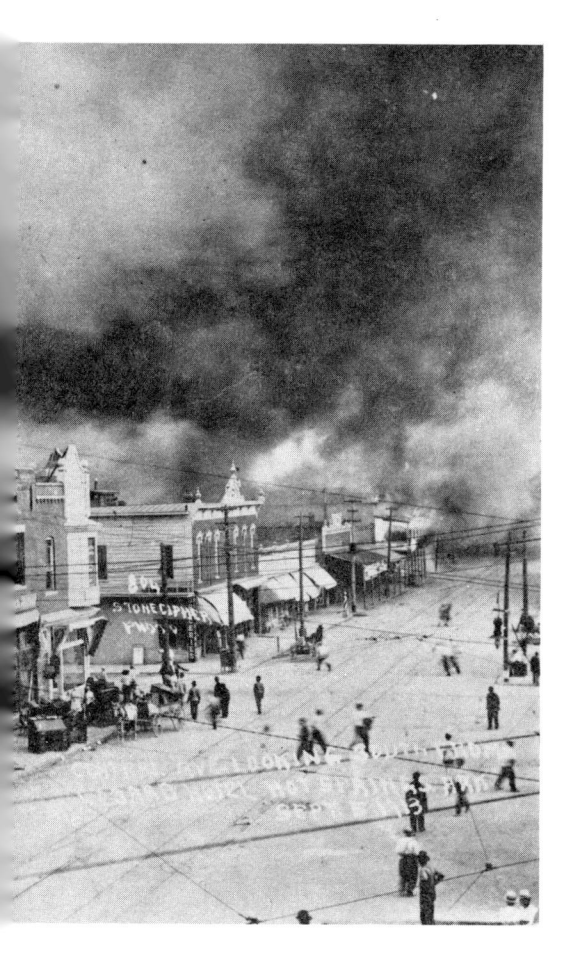

Above: Sarah Ellsworth. (Mary D. Hudgins Collection)

Right: Major P. H. Ellsworth, M.D. (Mary D. Hudgins Collection)

Although the city always seemed to be in a constant state of rebuilding (as it is now) some of the citizens usually found time to devote to improving the cultural side of life in the Spa. One of the early movers and shakers was Sarah Elizabeth Ellsworth, wife of Dr. Prosper Harvey Ellsworth, a leading physician. Although Dr. Ellsworth was born in Canada he had served as a surgeon with an Illinois regiment during the Civil War. He brought his Maryland bride to Hot Springs in 1873, and they eventually built "Wildwood," the elegant home that is still maintained on Park Avenue.

Interested in music, painting, and literature, Sarah Ellsworth gave as much time as she could spare from raising her four children to fostering the arts in her adopted town. For years the only library in Hot Springs was Hiram Whittington's personal collection, but in 1881 Mrs. Ellsworth and her friends founded a library association that was the beginning of the present excellent Tri-Lakes Regional Library.

Right: Residence of Dr. P. H. Ellsworth from *Cutter's Guide to the Hot Springs of Arkansas*, 1887. (Mary D. Hudgins Collection)

A few years ago, historian Mary D. Hudgins set out to compile a list of musicians and composers with Hot Springs connections, and the total was more than thirty, some of whom became well known in both the popular and classical fields. Two nationally known names in the world of music who lived in Hot Springs were Mary Lewis and Marjorie Lawrence. Soprano Mary Lewis, who learned to sing in churches, ran away to New York in 1919 to join the Ziegfeld Follies. Two years later she was the Follies' lead singer, but that was not good enough for Mary Lewis. She switched to grand opera, and throughout the 1920's performed both in America and abroad. In 1926 she returned to Hot Springs and gave an operatic concert at the Auditorium Theater. Ten years later she came home again for a few days to sing during the centennial observance of Saline County. "I'm enjoying being a country girl from Arkansas," she said, and hoped to return someday to stay. But Mary Lewis died six years later, aged only forty-one.

Australian-born Marjorie Lawrence, star of New York's Metropolitan Opera, came to the Spa after she was crippled by polio in 1941. She and her husband bought a home in Hot Springs and while still undergoing thermal treatments she started teaching a series of musical courses for young singers. During World War II, she traveled throughout the nation performing for servicemen's organizations, and in 1946 journeyed to Europe for other concerts. Each summer she always returned to her Hot Springs home to teach her popular opera workshops.

Above: Mary Lewis. (Mary D. Hudgins Collection)

Left: Marjorie Lawrence. (Mary D. Hudgins Collection)

Among those who made thermal bathing into an art were William G. Maurice and Jacques Manier. Maurice was one of the several St. Louisians who were early zealots for developing the Spa. At the age of eleven he acted as escort for his mother when she began visiting the Springs in 1870. Later in life Maurice remembered the enchantment the place had always held for him, and he returned in 1890 to build the first Maurice Bath House, replacing it in 1912 with the present handsome structure near the middle of Bath House Row.

In 1898, Jacques Manier arrived from Illinois to become assistant manager of the Maurice. During the next half century he was among the Spa's most ardent advocates of hot water therapy. "We Bathe the World" was a motto that he took to heart and strove continually to make others believe. To the townspeople Manier was affectionately known as the "Dean of Bath House Row."

A contemporary of Manier was William E. Chester, the "Dean of Hotel Managers." Born in Canada and educated in Buffalo, New York, Chester was only twenty-one when he came to Hot Springs to fill the night clerk's job in the swank Eastman Hotel. His abilities soon brought him the manager's position, and from there he went to the Arlington where he established his reputation as a hotel keeper par excellence.

In 1880 when he was about eight years old, John G. Lonsdale, a native of Memphis, Tennessee, came to the springs to live with an aunt, Mrs. J. P. Mellard. From his early twenties, Lonsdale was engaged in a number of enterprises beneficial to his adopted city. In 1899 he joined Samuel Fordyce in reorganizing the Little Rock, Hot Springs & Western Railroad. While the track was being completed, Lonsdale found a perfect site for a summer home in eastern Garland County. He called it "Peaceful Valley," and the railroad station nearby was given his name.

One of the town's leaders among its native-born inhabitants was David Burgauer, son of a German immigrant who came to Hot Springs in 1867. Born in 1873, Burgauer saw his town grow from a single-street village to a thriving Spa. Starting as a bookkeeper in a bank, he later helped found the Arkansas Trust Company and served as that institution's president for a quarter of a century before it became the present Arkansas Bank and Trust Company. Involved in almost every civic project in Hot Springs, Burgauer in his later years was usually greeted on the streets by young and old as "Uncle Dave."

Every city has some citizens who choose the spotlight of leadership, who may be likeable and colorful, yet who inspire contempt as well as admiration—exemplifying the old maxim that power corrupts and absolute power corrupts absolutely. Leo Patrick McLaughlin, born in 1892, grew up in Hot Springs during the prosperous period of "We Bathe the World." A year after he was admitted to the bar in 1912, he was into local politics, and was elected city attorney about the time he was old enough to vote.

In 1927 the voters chose McLaughlin to be their mayor and he held the office over the next twenty years, gradually uniting politics and illegal gambling until he developed a well-financed political machine that made it impossible for anyone to run for even the most minor of offices without the mayor's approval. McLaughlin was his own public relations man, and set out to create an image of happy-go-lucky cosmopolite, outfitting himself in sporty costumes, fancy hats, and riding britches. In public he always wore a red carnation in his lapel. Borrowing from Tom Cockburn's advertising stunt of a cart drawn by one of the Ostrich Farm's big birds running down Central Avenue and Madam Maxine's display of her girls in an open car, McLaughlin would hitch his fine horses named Scotch and Soda to a splendid cart and

Above: William G. Maurice. (Mary D. Hudgins Collection)

ride along the avenue waving at the passerbys like a king to his subjects.

The inhabitants who wanted their hometown to remain an "open city" admired McLaughlin and compared him to Jimmy Walker, the contemporary playboy mayor of New York City. In reality McLaughlin was more like the old-fashioned political bosses of Memphis, Kansas City, Chicago or Boston. He stayed in power by controlling the pay-offs of illegal gambling casinos, and by forcing those who depended upon his power to buy blocks of poll tax receipts, which at that time were prerequisites to voting in Arkansas. A visiting writer for *Redbook Magazine* charged that the poll tax receipts were handed out, with two-dollar bills attached, to "petty criminals, town drunks, and prostitutes" who then went willingly to the polls to vote for McLaughlin and his candidates. A local "madam" once claimed that she had to buy hundreds of poll tax receipts in order to stay in business.

In 1946, McLaughlin's machine was challenged by a returning Marine Corps officer, Sidney McMath, and several other veterans of World War II. Born in south Arkansas, McMath had grown up poor in Hot Springs—selling newspapers in gambling establishments, shining shoes, and boxing in amateur bouts. In the midst of the economic depression of the early 1930's, he hitch-hiked to Fayetteville with $2.50 in his pocket and started working his way through the University's law school. Like many of his immediate contemporaries, he was drawn into World War II before he could start a real career.

McMath and the other young veterans returning to Hot Springs had spent four years away from homes and families, putting their lives on the line to preserve democracy and the American way of life. But Mayor McLaughlin's way of life was not what they had been fighting for. In what the press described as the "G. I. Revolt," the veterans labeled the mayor "Der Fuehrer of Hot Springs" and began a campaign that was remindful in some ways of the Flynn-Doran gambling war, but with milder outbreaks of gunfire. (The full story of Sid McMath and the G. I. Revolt has been told in *A Man for Arkansas* by Jim Lester, and as has been previously noted, McLaughlin's political power was finally broken.) McMath won his campaign for prosecuting attorney, and he went on from there to become governor of Arkansas at 36, the youngest governor since the Civil War. Hot Springs, however, seems to grow politicians who mature at an early age. Bill Clinton, who spent his public school years in Hot Springs, was elected governor in 1978 at the age of 31, the youngest governor in the United States.

Of all the inhabitants who "wouldn't live anywhere else," Jefferson Davis Orear, the Arkansaw Thomas Cat, probably said it as well as anyone could: "I've had more fun than anybody in Hot Springs." For Christmas 1943, the old man printed up a little holiday message for his out-of-town friends, mailing it to them in a Thomas Cat wrapper done in bright red ink: "Everything is fine and lovely . . . roses and posies, cold pickles and nectarines . . . singing birds in every bush and happy smiles on happy faces . . . in Hot Springs, Ark., the Scenic Spot of Southland."

Above: Leo McLaughlin driving cart drawn by Scotch and Soda. (W. S. "Jay" Campbell)

CHAPTER VI
SOJOURNERS
"...no man need feel strange here."

In Hollywood they place the starred names of their famous people on a sidewalk. If Hot Springs should attempt to do this for the illustrious names who have trod the streets of the Spa during the past 150 years, the inlaid stars would fill all the promenades and sidewalks in town. Apparently everybody who is or was anybody visited Hot Springs at least once, and they still come to this magnetic city.

The first visitors came mainly to rid themselves of various ailments, and through the years some remarkable cures have been reported. "More than half the population of the place are cripples," geologist David Dale Owen noted in 1858, "either going with crutches or sticks and some of them have to be carried in litters to the baths." He was skeptical of the curative power of the springs, but admitted that healing had been effected in a number of cases.

In Judge William F. Pope's recollections of early days in Arkansas, he reported his first meeting with Roswell Beebe. Beebe was so incapacitated by rheumatism that he had to be carried off a New Orleans steamboat in a litter and transported by wagon to Hot Springs. "When I saw him a few months afterwards he was climbing all over the mountains, with the strength and agility of renewed youth."

Above: Roswell Beebe. (Arkansas History Commission)

Below: Hot Springs in 1858 from drawing by David Dale Owen, published in *Hot Springs Illustrated Monthly*, 1879. (Walter Nunn Collection)

A visitor of 1878 was struck by the number of extraordinary cures that had been accomplished by "a course of bathing in these pools, without the aid of medicine or a physician," and then he went on to suggest that the local doctors were giving too much medicine in conjunction with treatment by the waters. "The drug stores do an extremely thriving trade, and the amount of medicine seen in the rooms of your invalid friends is enough to sicken a well man."

Because so many visitors came in search of cures for ailments brought on by what was then described as "licentiousness," the impression got about that at least half the male sojourners in town were roues who had come to cure their burned out cases. But as one observer noted in 1878, "they become very quiet members of society while doing penance at the hot springs."

Even as recently as 1964, a visitor from New York complained that most of the talk he heard was about aches and pains. "Talk about aches and pains," he wrote, "has a never-ending quality, for it presents an infinite series of possible combinations; it can continue as long as it would take, say, all living Chinese to pass a given spot. The broad divisions of the pain-talk curriculum are location, frequency, duration, previous history, and prognosis. A chain reaction immediately sets in upon the porches, with one man's backache sliding naturally into another man's Charley horse."

Regardless of what topics were most popular as conversation pieces, it was the diversity of the sojourners that appealed to sensitive observers like Stephen Crane. "There will be mingled an accent from the South, a hat and pair of boots from the West, a hurry and important engagement from the North and a fine gown from the East. An advantage of this condition is that no man need feel strange here. He may assure himself that there are men of his kind present. If, however, he is mistaken and there are no men of his kind in Hot Springs he can conclude that his is a natural phenomenon and doomed to the curiosity of all peoples."

The first Very Important Person to visit Hot Springs after the departure of Hernando De Soto in 1541 must have been Sam Houston. In a letter dated July 13, 1833, Hiram Whittington noted proudly: "We have among us at this time the renowned General Houston, ex-Governor of Tennessee, ex-Aide de camp and bosom friend of General Jackson, ex-Indian chief, ex-Revolutionary General in Texas, etc." Before returning to Texas for greater glory, Houston spent a month at the Spa, bathing away a skin disease on his head.

Politicians and statesmen—including future, current and past Presidents—all loved to visit the Spa. Both Roosevelts came, Teddy to orate at the State Fair in 1910, Franklin D. to celebrate the Arkansas Centennial in 1936. F. D. R.'s wife Eleanor accompanied him, addressing the women of Hot Springs while he visited the Fordyce Bath House to observe thermal treatments of victims of polio—the affliction that had crippled him. Uncertainty still remains as to whether or not Roosevelt took a thermal bath during the visit. James (Big Jim) Farley, the postmaster-general who directed Roosevelt's political campaigns, also kept Hot Springs on his traveling circuit.

William Jennings Bryan, three-time loser as Democratic candidate for President, made his first visit in 1899, returning on numerous occasions and never failing to praise the waters of Hot Springs. The inhabitants learned to recognize him in his contemporary politician's uniform of long-tailed black alpaca coat, winged collar, and wide-brimmed hat.

In the year before his election as President, Herbert Hoover arrived to be honored at a banquet and receive a gold key to the

Above: Theodore Roosevelt from Reception Programme for the 1910 State Fair. (Arkansas History Commission)

Below: Franklin D. Roosevelt's visit to Hot Springs, 1936. (Garland Co. Historical Society)

Above: William Jennings Bryan. (Garland Co. Historical Society)

Below: Believed to be Al Capone and an unidentified friend drinking a beer in Happy Hollow. (Mark Palmer Collection)

Above: Herbert Hoover holding the key to Hot Springs. (Mary D. Hudgins Collection)

city. Louisiana's irrepressible Kingfish, Senator Huey Pierce Long, also received a key to the city in 1934 from the equally irrepressible Mayor Leo McLaughlin. Senator Long came to proclaim "every man a king" in Hot Springs as elsewhere. A year later he was gunned down in the capitol he ruled at Baton Rouge.

Three other politicians, all future Presidents at the times of their first visits, found the spa a delightful place to be. Harry Truman had a favorite club where he played his favorite game of poker for small stakes. According to legend, he also tipped small, one silver dime. While still a senator from Massachusetts, John Kennedy accepted Senator John McClellan's invitation in 1957 to address the Arkansas Bar Association's meeting at the Arlington. Lyndon Johnson, who would follow Kennedy to the Presidency, also came to address the Arkansas lawyers in convention, June 1962.

Outlaws Cole Younger and Jesse and Frank James came twice to rob stagecoaches on the Malvern Road. Many years afterward Cole returned to lecture against outlawry, and Frank returned to operate a concession stand at Happy Hollow. Al Capone and a host of mobster types, who were much more deadly than the James and Younger boys, used Hot Springs to relax in between wars over territorial rights to illegal booze, gambling and prostitution. Like warriors from the hostile Indian tribes who buried their hatchets while taking the hot baths, the mobsters buried their Tommy guns during their sojourn in the Spa.

William (Bat) Masterson, a law-and-order man from the Old West of Dodge City, liked Hot Springs so much that after the great fire of 1905, he devoted his energies to raising funds to rebuild the city and aid those who had lost everything.

Three women with widely different aims in life, who attracted considerable attention during their visits, were Carry Nation, Jane Addams and Helen Keller. When Carry arrived in 1905 her reputation as a smasher of saloons made the liquor dealers very nervous. Although she spoke against the evils of drink, handed out her pamphlets and flourished her hatchet, she was evidently more interested in finding a quiet place to settle down than in smashing whiskey bottles. But Hot Springs was probably too effervescent for Carry Nation; she later chose a smaller and quieter community in which to make her home—Eureka Springs in the Ozarks.

Jane Addams, Nobel prize winner and founder of Hull House in Chicago, came to spread her philosophy of social reform to improve the rights of women and children. Helen Keller, the remarkable blind deaf-mute who learned to read, write and talk, was drawn to Hot Springs by the presence of an uncle, Dr. James Keller, a nationally known surgeon. Miss Keller's first of several visits was in 1894 when she was only fourteen. Half a century later, in 1944, she came to the Army and Navy Hospital to encourage veterans blinded in World War II.

Athletes have always been attracted to the Spa. Many famed prize fighters have come to condition themselves with the thermal waters. The legendary John L. Sullivan and Jim Corbett were among the first in the 19th century, and Jess Willard always took the baths before beginning a strenuous season. Jack Dempsey, who knocked out Willard in 1919 to begin his colorful career during the 1920's, sometimes came with promoter Tex Willard. During the 1930's Primo Carnera, the Italian-born heavyweight champion, followed his predecessors' examples.

Billy Sunday came first as a baseball player and then as evangelist. On his first visit, Billy was aboard the Diamond Jo railroad train when it rounded a curve and came suddenly upon a blazing trestle. Unable to stop the locomotive, the engineer raced the cars across just seconds before the bridge collapsed. Afterwards Billy Sunday credited the near disaster as being one of the miraculous events in his life that led him to become a revivalist minister.

Almost a hundred years ago, baseball teams began coming to Hot Springs for spring training—which included taking the baths and drinking the mineral water as well as strengthening their muscles and sharpening their skills. The Chicago Cubs were first, working out on a makeshift field near where the Garland County Court House stands today. Except for a four-year lapse during World War I, the Pittsburgh Pirates trained every spring from 1901 through 1933. According to local baseball historians, the players were expected to drink "plenty of Mountain Valley water" every day of their stay.

Above: Helen Keller (right) with traveling companion Polly Thompson, 1944. (Mary D. Hudgins Collection)

Below: Carry Nation. (Mary D. Hudgins Collection)

Right and below: Interior of Opera House Bar and 1903 city directory entry referring to Carry Nation. (Garland Co. Historical Society)

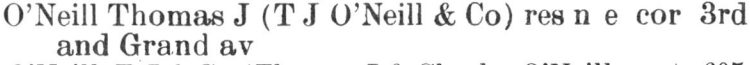

O'Neill Thomas J (T J O'Neill & Co) res n e cor 3rd and Grand av

O'Neill T J & Co (Thomas J & Charles O'Neill meats 605 Central av

Onion Club Roxie Merriwether pres H D Murray sec Opera House parlors

Opera House Bar Will H Estell prop (a place where all nations are welcome but Carrie) 102 Central av

Opera House The Grand J Frank Head mgr 100-106 Central av

Ora Marie dom Arlington hotel

Orear J Davis prop Ark Thomas Cat 105 Valley res

During this same period the Boston Red Sox also trained for several seasons at the Spa. The players used a ball park adjoining a zoo in Whittington Park and another that lay between the Ostrich and Alligator farms. On those rare days when the weather was too rainy for practice, the managers ordered the players to climb the mountains surrounding the town.

In 1913, Babe Ruth first arrived as a young pitcher with the Red Sox. In later years when he was a home-run slugger with the Yankees, he usually stopped by for a series of baths before joining his team elsewhere.

Among the great names of baseball who came either individually or with teams are Tris Speaker, Dizzy and Daffy Dean, Honus Wagner, Joe DiMaggio, Stan Musial, Rabbit Maranville, Lon Warneke, John McGraw and Rogers Hornsby, to name only a few. For a number of seasons, Hornsby ran a baseball school in Hot Springs.

Before Florida was invented and most of the teams went there to train, baseball fans could stroll through the lobby of the Majestic Hotel on any spring evening and see many of the great diamond stars of the day engaged in prankish antics, playing cards, or just relaxing in the comfortable chairs. In Florida if it rains, their successors have no mountains to climb and build up endurance, which may be one reason why baseball players of today are not as tough and long-lasting as they once were.

Right: Kate Smith with St. Louis Cardinals. (Mark Palmer Collection)

Below: Left to right: Jack Dempsey, Estelle Dempsey (wife) and Hiram Dempsey (father). (Mary D. Hudgins Collection)

Below: Dizzy Dean at the open display spring. (Mary D. Hudgins Collection)

Above: Will Rogers at Hot Springs (left to right) Frank Hawk (Rogers' pilot), Hamp Williams, Garnett Eisele, Mrs. Elise Avery Lake, Rogers, Fred Rix, and an unknown Chamber of Commerce official, 1931. (Mary D. Hudgins Collection)

Among the famous military men who found the Spa to their liking were two former enemies of the Civil War—Pierre Gustave Toutant de Beauregard and William Tecumseh Sherman. Beauregard came first, during the 1870's, while Sherman waited until Union heroes were old enough to also be viewed as heroes in the South. As commanding general of the U.S. Army he visited in March 1882. A hero to the nation in the months following World War I, General John J. Pershing received a tumultuous welcome when he arrived at the Rock Island depot February 13, 1920. As for the heroes of World War II and later conflicts, those who have come for reasons of health are far too numerous to mention.

Tycoons, the giants of commerce and industry, have always been frequenters of luxury hotels and bath houses. Jay Gould, who reputedly kept the first dollar he earned until the day he died, visited the first time at the invitation of Diamond Jo Reynolds. A railroad financier, Gould had a town named for him on one of his lines in southeast Arkansas, as well as half of *Paragould*, in northeast Arkansas. Philip Armour, the millionaire meat packer of Chicago, and F. W. Woolworth, creator of five-and-ten-cent stores, both proclaimed the benefits they obtained from thermal baths. Andrew Carnegie, who seemed to enjoy distributing his money as well as making it in the steel industry, also found the waters of the Spa restful in the last years of his busy life.

As for entertainers—actors, musicians, dancers, singers, magicians—so many have performed or relaxed in Hot Springs that a listing of them would become a catalog. They began back in the days of the old Opera House with names out of stage history— Joseph Jefferson, Lillian Russell and Evelyn Nesbit down through John Barrymore and Douglas Fairbanks, Sr. to the latest meteoroids from Las Vegas and the television studios. Suffice it to say that entertainers who have not played in Hot Springs must have not yet made it, as they say, into the "big time."

Below: Lillian Russell. (Mark Palmer Collection)

Above: Jay Gould. (Arkansas History Commission)

INDEX

Acree, W. M., 67.
Addams, Jane, 92.
Airplanes, 26.
Alligator Farm, 72, 73, 93.
Allison, John, 51.
American Turf Assn., 60.
Amity, Ark., 21.
Anderson, Chas. T., 15.
Animal Wonderland, 72.
Anselberg, David, 70.
Arkadelphia, Ark., 18.
Arkansas Bank and Trust Company, 77, 87.
Arkansas Bar Association, 97.
Arkansas Centennial, 44, 90.
Arkansas Club, 53.
Arkansas Derby, 60.
Arkansas Gazette, 13, 20, 45, 59.
Arkansas Jockey Club, 60.
Arkansas National Bank, 77.
Arkansas State Fair, 26, 61, 72.
Arkansas Trust Company, 77, 87.
Arkansaw Thomas Cat, 76.
Armour, Philip, 94.
Army and Navy Hospital, 37, 40, 67, 77, 92.
Auditorium Theater, 48, 49, 86.
Axum, Donna, 72.

Banking, 77.
Baptist Church, 78, 83.
Barnes, Phineas, 81.
Barnum, Phineas, 47.
Barrymore, John, 94.
Bartholomew, John, 21.
Baseball, 92-93.
Batesville, Ark., 15.
Bath house, first, 28.

Bath House Row, 32, 33, 35, 36, 37, 42, 43, 52, 63, 64, 76, 78, 81, 87.
Bath houses
  Alhambra, 35.
  Big Iron, 33, 35.
  Buckstaff, 35, 43.
  Fordyce, 44, 90.
  Free, 32, 38, 39, 43, 77.
  Hale, 28, 32, 35, 37, 43.
  Horseshoe, 35, 43.
  Hot Springs, 35.
  Imperial, 40, 43.
  Independent, 35.
  Ladies, 32.
  Lamar, 35, 43, 70.
  Magnesia, 32, 35, 43.
  Maurice, 43, 87.
  Mud Hole, 39.
  New Rector, 35.
  Ozark, 32, 35, 37, 43.
  Palace, 32, 33, 35, 44, 52.
  Park, 35.
  Quapaw, 43.
  Rammelsberg, 35, 37, 43, 52.
  Rector, 29, 32.
  Rockafellow, 35.
  Superior, 35.
Bathing, 9, 28, 33, 34, 37, 81.
Beauregard, Pierre G., 94 (portrait).
Beebe, Roswell, 89 (portrait).
Belasco, David, 47.
Belding, George, 13, 17, 59.
Belding, Ludovicus, 12 (portrait), 13, 14, 16, 28, 63.
Belvedere Club, 57.
Benton, Ark., 15.
Blakely Mountain, 82.
B'nai Brith, 77.

Borland, Frank, 51.
Borland, Solon, 15 (portrait).
Bryan, William Jennings, 90, 91 (portrait).
Burbank, John, 19.
Burgauer, David, 77 (portrait), 87.
Burke, Billie, 47.
Business Men's League, 61.
Butterfield, David A., 22-23.

Caddo Gap, Ark., 15, 21.
Caddo Indians, 9, 11.
Caldwell, H. C., 15.
Calion, Ark., 10.
Camden, Ark., 10.
Campbell, H. L., 72.
Capone, Al, 52, 91 (portrait).
Carnegie, Andrew, 94.
Carnera, Primo, 92.
Cates, Isaac, 11.
Catholic Church, 78.
Cella, Charles, 62.
Cella, Louis, 59, 60.
Central Theater, 48.
Chamberlain, Dr., 67 (portrait).
Chase, William, 16.
Chase, Mrs. William, 16.
Cherokee Indians, 14.
Chester, William F., 87.
Choctaw Railroad, 59.
Churches, 12, 78, 83.
Civil War, 15, 78, 85.
Clinton, Bill, 88.
Cockburn, Edwin, 72 (portrait).
Cockburn, Thomas, 72, 87.
Cockburn, Mrs. Thomas, 72 (portrait).
Columbus, Harry, 58.
Committee of Twelve, 53.
Connell, W. H., 26.

Aerial view of Hot Springs at the turn of the century. (Arkansas History Commission)

Conway, James, 63.
Cooper, Simon, 60.
Corbett, Jim, 92.
Crane, Stephen, 24, 36, 37, 38, 90.
Crump, George R., 18-19.
Cugat, Xavier, 57.
Cupp, Cecil, Sr., 77 (portrait).
Curtiss, Glenn, 26.
Cutter, Charles, 75 (portrait).
Cutter's Guide to Hot Springs, 64, 81.

Dale, Tom, 51.
Davis, Jeff, 54.
Davis, Lynn, 58, 59.
Davis, Will J., 67 (portrait).
Dean, Daffy, 93.
Dean, Dizzy, 93 (portrait).
Dempsey, Estelle Taylor, 93 (portrait).
Dempsey, Jack, 92, 93 (portrait).
DeSoto, Hernando, 10, 49, 90.
"Diamond Jo" Railroad (see Hot Springs Railroad)
DiMaggio, Joe, 93.
"Doctor drummers," 41.
Doran, S. A., 50-54, 58.
Drew, John, 47.
Dunbar, Wm., 10 (portrait), 11.
Dwight Mission, 14.

Eisele, Martin, 41, 80 (portrait).
El Paso Stage Lines, 20-21.
Ellsworth, Prosper Harvey, 85 (portrait).
Ellsworth, Sarah Elizabeth, 20, 85 (portrait).
Erickson, S. J., 26.
Essex Park, 59-62.

Fairbanks, Douglas Sr., 94.
Farley, James, 90.
Faubus, Orval, 56, 58.
Featherstonhaugh, George, 12, 14, 17, 18.
Fields, Charles, 80.
Fires, 82-84.
First National Bank, 78.
Flanagin, Harris, 15.
Floods, 82, 84, 85.
Flynn, Billy, 51, 53 (portrait).
Flynn, Frank, 50, 51, 52, 53 (portrait), 54, 55, 58.
Flynn, Jack, 51, 52.
Fordyce, Samuel W., 23, 25 (caricature), 40, 44, 46, 63-67, 82, 87.
Fountains, 42-43.
French Restaurant, 82.

"G.I. Revolt," 88.
Gaines, William H., 16 (portrait), 18, 63, 67.
Gambling, 50-59.
Garland County, 15.
Garland County Court House, 26, 83, 92.
Garnett, Algernon, S., 40.
Gillis, "California Jack," 21.
Gould, Jay, 94 (portrait).
Greenleaf's Bagnio, 82.
Green, Peter E., 82.
Greenville, Ark., 18.
Gulpha Creek, 11, 18, 21.

Haggerty, Capt., 28.
Hale, John Cyrus, 16, 28, 29, 78.
Hale, Sarah, 78.
Hamblen, Samuel, 38, 80.
Hamburger, Philip, 57-58.
Hammond, William J., 81.
Happy Hollow, 70, 71, 72, 91.
Harris, Dane, 55, 56.
Harris, Maxine, 56, 87.
Harrison, William, 15.
Head, Frank, 48 (portrait).
Hedwig, Charlotte, 43.
Hellwigg, F. F., 43.
Higgins, John, 75.
Hoover, Herbert, 90, 91 (portrait).
Hornet, The, 75.
Hornsby, Rogers, 93.
Horseracing, 59-62.
Horseshoe, The, 53, 75.

Hotels
  Arlington, 25, 36, 49, 52, 63, 64, 66, 67, 68, 69, 82, 83, 87, 91.
  Avenue, 64, 65, 68.
  Earl, 63.
  Eastman, 67, 68, 87.
  Grand Central, 83.
  Hale, 28, 63.
  Hay House, 64, 65.
  Hot Springs, 25, 32, 63, 83.
  Majestic, 14, 68, 93.
  Park, 34, 68, 69, 84.
  Plateau, 83.
  Rector House, 29, 31, 63, 64.
  Stidham's 29, 63.
  United States, 64, 66.
  Visitor's Home, 52.
  Waverly, 64, 65.

Hot Springs Airport Company, 26.
Hot Springs Airship Company, 26.
Hot Springs Clay Products Co., 74.
Hot Springs Courier, 75.
Hot Springs Creek, 12, 13, 30, 36, 80, 82, 84.
Hot Springs Daily Sentinel, 83.
Hot Springs "diamonds," 81.
Hot Springs Electric Company, 77.
Hot Springs Federal Reservation, 16.
Hot Springs Fire Dept., 83.
Hot Springs Illustrated Monthly, 75.
Hot Springs Jockey Club, 59, 60.
Hot Springs Mountain Tower, 71.

Hot Springs "New Era," 26, 75.
Hot Springs News, 75.
Hot Springs Post Office, 23, 67, 83.
Hot Springs Railroad, 20-21, 23, 24, 25, 40, 53, 59, 92.
Hot Springs Record, 75.
Hot Springs Sentinel, 71, 75.
Hot Springs Street Railroad, 23, 25, 84.
Hot Springs Times, 75.
Houston, Sam, 90.
Howell, Ed, 51.
Hudgins, Mary D., 41, 86.
Hunter, George, 10, 11.
Hurst, Q. Byrum, 54 (portrait), 59.
Hutson, J. D., 75.

I.Q. Zoo, 72.
Iron Mountain Railroad, 17, 21, 22, 25, 30, 64.
Iron Mountain Railroad Depot, 74.

Jackson, Andrew, 14.
James, Frank, 91.
James, Jesse, 20 (portrait), 21, 91.
Jebb, Frank, 34.
Jefferson, Joseph, 47, 94.
Jefferson, Thomas, 10.
Johnson, Jim, 58.
Johnson, Lyndon, 91.

Keller, Helen, 92 (portrait).
Keller, James, 92.
Kelley, Benj. F., 38, 80.
"Kelleytown", 38, 80.
Kennedy, John, 91.

Lake Catherine, 62.
Lane, Abbe, 57.
Lane, Jim, 50, 83.
Lansing, Harry, 51.
Latta, G. G., 82.
Lawrence, Marjorie, 86 (portrait).
Lawrence, Station, 59.
Lemon, Sarah, 12.
Leo N. Levi Memorial Hospital, 77.
Lester, Jim, 88.
Lewis, Mary, 86 (portrait).
Libbey, Donald S., 80.
Libbey Memorial Physical Medicine Center, 39, 77, 80.
Libraries, 13, 14, 85.
Little Rock, Ark., 13, 15, 16, 17, 18, 25, 60, 72, 84.
Little Rock, Hot Springs and Western Railroad, 25, 81.
Little, William J., 41, 42, 77, 80.
Logan, John H., 40.
Long, Huey Pierce, 91.
Long, Stephen H., 12, 27.
Lonsdale, John G., 87.
Lott, Uriah, 25.
Lucius, Jake, 51.
"Lum and Abner," 49.

McClellan, John, 91.
McGraw, John, 93.
McGuigan, Wm., 60.
McLaughlin, Leo Patrick, 55 (portrait), 87, 88 (portrait), 91.
McLeod, Norman, 70 (caricature).
McMath, Sidney, 54 (portrait), 88.
McTague, Billy, 52.

Madden, Vincent Owen, 55, 56.
Malvern, Ark., 11, 15, 18-22, 24, 40, 53, 63, 64, 91.
Magic Springs Family Fun Park, 72, 73.
Magnet Cove, Ark., 17.
Munier, Jacques, 80.
Maranville, Rabbit, 93.
Masterson, William (Bat), 91.
Maurice, Wm. G., 67 (portrait), 87 (portrait).
Mellard, Joseph, 12, 28, 63.
Mellard, Mrs. T. P., 87.
Mellard, Nancy, 12, 28, 63.
Memphis, Dallas & Gulf Railroad, 25.
Methodist Church, 78, 83, 84.
Mid-America Center, 74.
Miller, Clell, 21.
Miss Arkansas Pageant, 72.
Missouri Pacific Railroad, 25.
Mitchell, Jacob, 29.
Mount Ida, Ark., 15.
Mountain Valley Water, 82, 92.
Murfreesboro, Ark., 21.
Musgrove, W. G., 75.
Musial, Stan, 93.
Musicians and Composers, 86.

Natchez Indians, 9.
Natchitoches Indians, 11.
Nation, Carry, 92 (portrait).
Nesbit, Evelyn, 47, 94.
Newspapers, 75.
Noble, John, 42.
Novaculite, 9, 81.
Nutt, Sidney, 49 (portrait).

Oaklawn Park, 26, 59-62, 72.
O'Neill, James, 47.
Opera House, 46-48, 92.
Orear, Jefferson Davis, 76 (portrait), 88.
Osage Indians, 9.
Ostrich Farm, 56, 72, 87, 93.
Ouachita Mountains, 11.
Ouachita Pottery Co., 74.
Ouachita River, 10, 11, 27, 46.
Owen, David Dale, 89.
Ozark Sanitarium, 84.

Patti, Adelina, 48.
Percival, John, 11, 12, 16, 28.
Pershing, John J., 94.
Pinkerton, William, 67 (portrait).
Pope, William F., 89.

Population, 15.
Pottery, 74.
Presbyterian Church, 78.
Princess Theater, 49.
Prudhomme, Jean Emanuel, 11, 12 (portrait).
Pruitt, Bob and Dave, 51.

Quapaw Indians, 9.

Radio & television, 49.
Railroads, 21-22, 24, 25.
Reagan, Thos. J., 28.
Rector, Elias, 29.
Rector, Henry M., 15 (portrait), 16, 18, 29, 63.
Rehabilitation Center, 40.
Reservation Police, 81.
Reyburn, Samuel, 63.
Reynolds, Joseph, 22 (portrait), 23, 24, 94.
Rice, Joel T., 26.
Riggs, John A., 26 (portrait), 75.
Roads & trails, 17, 26.
Robinson, Jos. T., 49.
Rock Island Railroad, 25.
Rockafellow, Charles N., 79 (portrait).
Rockefeller, Winthrop, 56, 58-59.
Rockport, Ark., 15, 21.
Rogers, Will, 94 (portrait).
Rooney, Mickey, 50.
Roosevelt, Eleanor, 90.
Roosevelt, Franklin D., 90 (portrait).
Roosevelt, Theodore, 41, 72, 90 (portrait).
Royal, Ark., 26.
Rusk, Howard A., 45.
Russell, Lillian, 47, 94 (portrait).
Ruth, Babe, 93.

Saline County, 86.
Schlafley family, 82.
"Scotch and Soda," 87, 88.
Scripps, John, 12.
Sevier, Ambrose, 14 (portrait).
Sherman, William T., 94.
Smith, Alta, 44.
Smith, Kate, 93 (portrait).
Southern Club, 56-58.
Spas, 29, 30.
Speaker, Tris, 93.
Sportsman Park, 59.
Springs:
  Alum, 31.
  Arlington, 42.
  Arsenic, 30, 33, 42.
  Big Iron, 27, 33.
  Corn Hole, 31, 32.
  Egg, 31.
  Kidney, 31.
  Liver, 31, 42.
  Magnesia, 30, 31, 42.
  Mountain Valley, 16, 82.
  Mud, 31, 38, 39, 42.
  Pool of Bethesda, 31.
  Sulphur and Iron, 31, 42.
Stagecoach robberies, 18, 19, 20, 21.
Stagecoaches, 18-19, 20, 21.
Stearns, Frank, 82, 83.
Stevens, Wm., 12.
Stitt, Samuel, 63, 64 (portrait), 67, 82.
Sullivan, John L., 92.
Sulphur Creek, 11.
Sumpter, John, 81.
Sunday, Billy, 92.

Texarkana, Ark., 21.
Thaw, Harry K., 47.
Theaters, 46, 47, 48.
Thompson, Asa, 28, 29.
Thompson, Frank, 80.
Thompson, Polly, 92 (portrait).
Tiny Town, 72.
Toler, Tom, 52.
Tower Club, 56, 58.
Tri-Lakes Regional Library, 85.
Truman, Harry, 91.
Tunica Indians, 9.
Tussaud's Wax Museum, 72.

U.S. National Park Service, 39, 42.
U.S. Public Health Service, 39.
U.S. Veterans Bureau, 40.
U.S. War Depart., 40.

Valachi, Joseph, 56.
Vapors Club, 55, 56, 57, 58.

Wagner, Honus, 93.
Walker, Jimmy, 88.
Ward, Elizabeth, 72.
Warde, Frederick, 46.
Warneke, Lon, 93.
Washington, Ark., 17.
Western Jockey Club, 59, 60.
White, Stanford, 47.
Whittington, Emma, 25 (portrait).
Whittington, Hiram Abiff, 13, 14 (portrait), 25, 68, 72, 77, 80-81, 85, 90.
Whittington, Mary Burnham, 14.
Whittington Park, 26, 72, 73, 93.
"Wildwood," 85.
Willard, Tex, 92.
Willard, Jess, 92.
Woodruff, Wm., 13.
Woolman, Ellis, 71.
Woolworth, F. W., 94.

Younger brothers, 20 (portraits), 21, 91.

Ziegfeld Follies, 86.

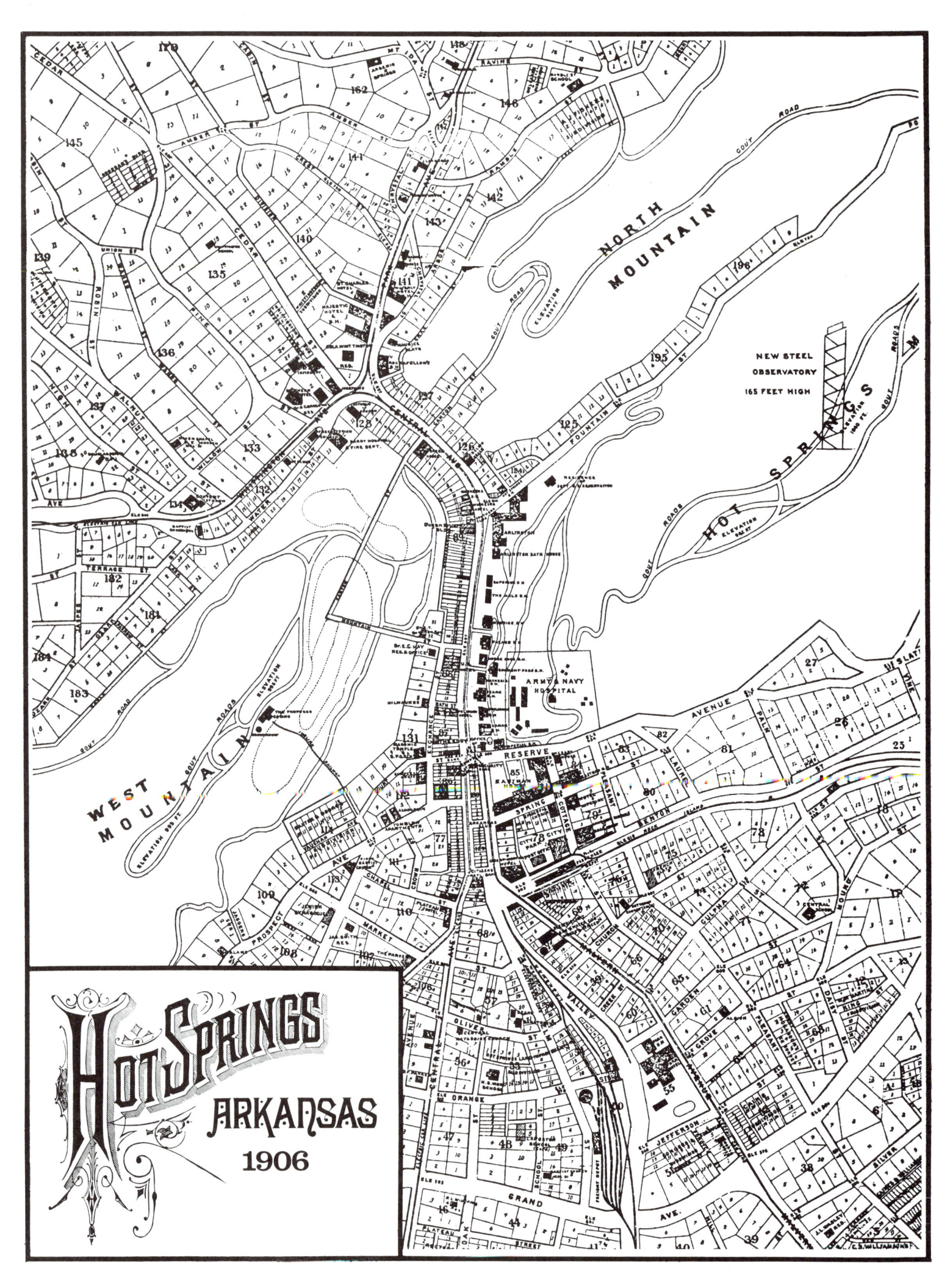

Hot Springs Arkansas 1906